Malherbe, Théophile de Viau, and Saint-Amant

AF305171

Manchester University Press

Malherbe, Théophile de Viau, and Saint-Amant
A selection

Edited, with an introduction and notes
by R. G. Maber

Manchester University Press

Manchester and New York

Copyright © R. G. Maber 1983, 1991, 2009

The right of R. G. Maber to be identified as the editor of this work has been asserted by him in accordance with the Copyright, Designs and Patents Act 1988.

Published by Manchester University Press
Oxford Road, Manchester M13 9NR, UK
and Room 400, 175 Fifth Avenue, New York, NY 10010, USA
www.manchesteruniversitypress.co.uk

Distributed exclusively in the USA by
Palgrave, 175 Fifth Avenue, New York NY 10010, USA

Distributed exclusively in Canada by
UBC Press, University of British Columbia, 2029 West Mall,
Vancouver, BC, Canada V6T 1Z2

British Library Cataloguing-in-Publication Data
A catalogue record for this book is available from the British Library

Library of Congress Cataloging-in-Publication Data
A catalog record for this book is available from the Library of Congress

ISBN 13: 978 0 7190 8188 0

First published 1983 by Durham Modern Languages Series
Second, revised edition pubished 1991 by Durham Modern Languages Series
This edition first published 2009 by Manchester University Press

Printed by Lightning Source

Preface

This volume has its origins in a selection of texts (*Six French Poets of the Seventeenth Century*) that has been used for the past five years with first-year Honours undergraduates in Durham, and was prompted by the success that the poetry of this period enjoyed with readers who were relative newcomers to French verse. Its aim is modest: to give as representative a selection of the work of the three poets concerned as is possible in a restricted compass, together with sufficient supporting documentation to bring out the unique literary personality of each, and to help to render the poetry as accessible as possible to a modern reader. It is thus designed to fill the gap between the scholarly complete editions and the more general anthologies of seventeenth-century poetry, which are rarely able to devote much space to any one author. Severe limitations of space have made it impossible to give anything like a comprehensive overall picture of the development of poetry during this interesting period, or to provide more than brief notes to the poems. However, there is a short bibliography at the end with suggestions for further reading.

Unlike most anthologies, this selection contains, as far as possible, complete poems; only five out of the thirty-six poems printed here are incomplete, in each case because the whole work was too long for inclusion. Thus although some of the poems might seem to be rather more uneven than they sometimes appear when only carefully-chosen extracts are read, this does mean that their aesthetic integrity is preserved, and it offers a more accurate view of their author's work.

Preface to the Second Edition

In this revised edition the choice of texts and pagination of the poems have been left unchanged, to avoid difficulties where it is used as a course text. However, the notes have been extended and the bibliography augmented and updated; and the text has been corrected throughout.

Table of Contents

INTRODUCTION

The first half of the seventeenth century is an exceptionally rich and complex time in French poetry. There are a number of highly gifted writers who produced fine poetry in many different genres, and in addition an abundance of talented minor figures whose works have a remarkable diversity. There is a general mood of modernism in poetry: a sense that previously-accepted conventions have had their day, and that the new world of the seventeenth century –political and social, as well as literary– demands appropriate new forms of expression. This led, not to uniformity, but to a great deal of experimentation in verse, as different poets cultivated their art in very dissimilar ways.

The three poets represented here, Malherbe, Théophile de Viau, and Saint-Amant, are among the most outstanding literary personalities of their time. All three enjoyed great popularity among their contemporaries, and yet they are strikingly different one from another in almost every respect – in character and ideas, in the circumstances of their lives, and, perhaps most importantly, in their attitudes to their art. As we shall see, each developed a strong personal style based on quite different principles; and while the choice of each can be justified simply in terms of the quality of his literary achievement, they are made all the more interesting by the contrasts beween them.

FRANÇOIS DE MALHERBE

François de Malherbe was born in Caen in 1555, and after an excellent education was appointed 'secrétaire' to the Governor of Provence, Henri d'Angoulême, illegitimate son of Henri II. He spent nine years in Provence (1576-85), then ten years in Caen before returning to Provence in 1595. A curious feature of his life is that he did not seem to find his true path in poetry until his mid-forties, a relatively advanced age for a poet. He apparently did not write a great deal of poetry before about 1595, and with few exceptions what has survived is either much inferior to his later work or of a quite different kind – most strikingly so in the case of his one long early poem, *Les Larmes de Saint Pierre* (1587), a florid and hyperbolic religious work imitated from the Italian of Luigi Tansillo. His abilities were first seriously noted in 1600, when he wrote a celebratory poem for the arrival in Aix of the new queen, Marie de Médicis, and the decisive change in his life occurred five years later, when he came to Paris in the *suite* of his friend, the great humanist magistrate and neo-stoic philosopher Guillaume Du Vair. Here he devoted his forceful personality to establishing both his artistic principles and his personal position, and definitively confirmed the success of both with his fine ode, *Prière pour le Roi allant en Limousin*, of November 1605. He set himself up in direct opposition to the prevailing style of court poetry, that 'style doux-coulant' whose most celebrated exponent was then the aging Desportes, and rapidly rose to the greatest literary eminence. He became accepted as the leading court poet to Henri IV and the Regency, and was also the head of a school of admiring younger poets, the most gifted of whom were Maynard and Racan (who left a manuscript life of Malherbe, full of picturesque anecdotes). Even though his personal role was less exalted after about 1615, he retained his extraordinary prestige for the rest of his life. He kept his powers to the end, his final great state poem, *Pour le Roi, allant châtier la rébellion des Rochellois*, being finished in early 1628; but during his last years a new note of disillusion and bitterness can also be felt at times in his poetry, a sense that he had not received his due from the great whose praises he had extolled (e.g. his *Paraphrase du Psaume CXLV*). A serious blow came in 1627, with the death in a duel of his son, Marc-Antoine. He devoted all his energies to bringing the young man's killers to justice, even following the king to the siege of La Rochelle in 1628 to press his case; but the effort proved too much for him, and, returning to Paris at the end of September, he died on 6 December 1628 of a fever contracted during the journey.

Malherbe's poetic output does not lack variety, and the poems included in this edition illustrate most of the major categories into which his work can be divided. Thus we have the great official odes (one of the earliest, *Prière pour le Roi Henri le Grand, allant en Limousin*, pp. 7-10, and the last, *Pour le Roi, allant châtier la rébellion des Rochellois*, pp. 18-23); verses for royal ballets, which often had some political significance (*Prophétie du Dieu de Seine*, p. 17); consolations (*Consolation à Monsieur Du Périer*, pp. 3-6); love poems, which can be subdivided into commissioned ones for his patrons (the poems *Pour Alcandre*, pp. 11-12 and 12-14), and apparently personal ones (*Dessein de quitter une dame*, p. 6, *Chanson (Sonnet)*, pp. 14-15, and probably the *Chanson*, pp. 15-16); some religious verse (*Paraphrase du Psaume CXLV*, pp. 24-25); and a wide range of other short personal poems, occasional verse, and epigrams (two epigrams, pp. 16-17, *Au Roi*, pp. 17-18, *Sur la mort de son fils*, p. 24).

In everything he does, Malherbe's poetry is highly distinctive, and deliberately so; in order to appreciate it fully it is important to be aware of certain fundamental attitudes and principles that underlie all the work of his maturity, and had an immense influence for generations after his death. He was concerned above all with clarity, precision, and careful craftsmanship in poetry. In language and style, the guide should be general usage, and the attempt of the Pléiade poets and their followers to enrich their vocabulary with neologisms, archaisms, and dialect words, is firmly rejected, as is any eccentricity or gratuitous obscurity in imagery or Classical allusions. The details of versification to which he most strongly objected are all the marks of careless or over-facile composition – features such as, in particular, internal rhymes, hiatus, displacement of the caesura, unnecessary *enjambement*, ambiguity of expression, and feeble or hackneyed rhymes. However, in Malherbe's self-appointed role as the reformer of French verse something more basic is involved than matters of language and technique; this concerns the whole concept of the poet, his inspiration, and his function in society. For Ronsard, continuing a tradition going back to Pindar, the poet is the divinely inspired seer, or *vates*, who is transported by his inspiration –the *furor poeticus*– to attain truths inaccessible to ordinary mortals, and who can thus justify the highest and noblest claims for his art. To this Malherbe opposed a view which is essentially that of the poet as master-craftsman (an 'excellent arrangeur de syllabes', as he said to Racan), and he brought a robust, common-sense approach to the more extravagant claims of poetic inspiration (see Appendix, p. 72). Yet the poet does have a positive social role to play. He gives the grandest and noblest expression to the achievements of the king and presents his contemporaries with an idealized vision of the state, and thus in his way helps in the great work of reconstruction after the disastrous civil wars of the previous century; and, as Malherbe was fond of pointing out, he has the power to bestow immortal fame on his patrons (*Sonnet*, pp. 17-18; *Pour le Roi, allant châtier la rébellion des Rochellois*, lines 137-60). This idea is itself little more than a commonplace, but it is given new emphasis by its presentation here as one of the proper functions of state poetry.

Malherbe came to be seen by later critics as something of a watershed in the development of French poetry, and Boileau's famous lines in his *Art poétique* of 1673, 'Enfin Malherbe vint . . .', express a view widely held at the time. However, in spite of this, and his own skilful self-advertisement, his theory and practice were not in fact wholly revolutionary. Rather, his so-called 'reforms' continue and intensify a tendency which is already evident in the poets of the previous generation (many of whom, of course, were actually near-contemporaries of his), such as Du Perron, Desportes –who was to be the particular butt of Malherbe's criticism– and especially Bertaut. This tendency, which had been a gradual and only half-realized evolution, came to crystallize in the person of Malherbe, and he compelled attention and respect because of the strength of his personality, the quality of his own poetry, and the ruthlessness of his criticism of the work of others. He never embarked on any systematic Art of Poetry to expound his theories; he propagated them through his poetry itself, providing literary models that were imitated for decades, and equally importantly, through negative criticism of other poets, delivered orally or in marginal notes to his copies of their works, and eagerly absorbed by his followers. His criticisms of Desportes are the most important of all. He was probably intending to publish a detailed critique of Desportes's poems, but abandoned it on the older poet's death in 1606; however, his own copy of the work has survived with its copious annotations, and it well illustrates both his extreme meticulousness and, one must admit, the justice of many of his objections. It is very interesting to see exactly what features Malherbe objected to in poetry, as it helps us to understand the principles that govern the nature of his own work; for this reason, a selection of his annotations is given, with comments, in the Appendix, pp. 70-72.

Malherbe's concern for mastery of form is clear in all the poetry of his maturity. Because of the great importance of this feature of his work, and his profound influence on the development of French poetry (even among poets who consciously rejected his view of his art), it is worth considering certain aspects of this in some detail. The best place to begin is with his handling of the alexandrine. Malherbe developed more thoroughly than any previous poet the potentiality of the twelve-syllable line as a vehicle for serious and elevated statement, and it is not too fanciful to see in his poetry the model from which ultimately evolved the alexandrines of classical tragedy (it is interesting, too, to note in passing that the alexandrine used in comedy –by Molière above all, but by many other playwrights including Racine in *Les Plaideurs*– is freer, less elevated and more flexible, and, as we shall see, can in many ways be compared with the use of the line by Théophile and Saint-Amant).

The typical Malherbian alexandrine is end-stopped; he does sometimes use *enjambement*, in spite of his theoretical disapproval of it, but it is always consciously employed for deliberate effect. The line has a strongly-marked caesura after the sixth syllable, and each half of the line also commonly has a slighter pause in the rhythm, most usually after the third and ninth syllables, to give a perfectly balanced pattern of 3 + 3 // 3 + 3:

Ta douleur, du Périer, sera donc éternelle?

The many possible variations of this pattern (2 + 4, 4 + 2, etc.) are very frequently used to give relative prominence to the shorter rhythmic phrase of the half-line, as when he emphasizes the subject of the opening invocation in two of his most famous poems, written at opposite ends of his career:

Beauté, / mon beau souci, // de qui l'âme / incertaine . . .

N'espérons plus, / *mon âme*, // aux promess/es du monde . . .

A particularly striking example is found in the powerful opening to the *Prophétie du Dieu de Seine*:

Va-t'en / à la malheure, // excrément / de la terre,
Mon/stre qui dans la paix // fais les maux / de la guerre . . .

Such a form is obviously particularly well suited to striking a balance or pointing a contrast between the two halves of the line (made far more effective, of course, by the avoidance of *enjambement*), and a very large number of Malherbe's most celebrated lines depend for much of their effect on his use of chiasmus, the symmetrical placing of words and sounds. Thus the opening line of *Pour Alcandre*, 'Revenez, mes plaisirs, ma dame est revenue', not only strikes a verbal balance between the first and last words, but also, through this, establishes an implied equation between 'mes plaisirs' and 'ma dame' (the whole point of the poem); and, as the shortest phrase of the line, the greatest prominence is appropriately given to 'ma dame'. Another particularly successful example may be found in the justly famous lines in the *Consolation à Du Périer*:

Et rose, elle a vécu ce que vivent les roses,
    L'espace d'un matin.

The basic idea here is a simple parallel between the beauty and short life of the girl and that of a rose, very familiar through centuries of poetry; yet it is here dramatically renewed by being introduced with a startling metaphor in apposition (not 'elle était comme une rose' or even 'elle était une rose', but 'rose, elle . . .'). The chiasmus in this line is almost perfect, the two halves forming a balance not only of sense (rose . . . vécu / vivent . . . roses) but also of sound (Et *rose elle* a *vécu* ce *que vivent les roses*). This line is not the result of a happy stroke of inspiration, but the culmination of a typically long and deliberate evolution. In the first version of the poem, called *Consolation à Cléophon*, c. 1589-1595, the girl concerned was called Rosette, which provided the point of the lines:

Et ne pouvait Rosette être mieux que les roses
    Qui ne vivent qu'un jour.

Du Périer's daughter was called Marguerite, so the link between her and the rose has become purely metaphorical, as opposed to the much weaker comparison used earlier. The thought has been concentrated in every way, and, equally, the technical improvement in the lines is immense, and a fine example of what can be achieved by the laborious processes of the poet-craftsman.

As can be seen from lines such as these, Malherbe possessed an outstanding awareness of the harmonic possibilities of the language, and this is the aspect of his art singled out for particular praise by contemporaries (see the comments of Guez de Balzac and, rather later, Boileau, in the Appendix, pp. 73 and 77). As his annotations to Desportes show, he had an acutely sensitive ear for cacophonous or potentially comic juxtapositions of sounds, and such defects are scrupulously avoided in his own work. On the other hand, one often finds patterns of assonance or repeated consonants giving a firm sense of structure to a stanza, and subtly reinforcing its sense. Thus in the last stanza of the same *Consolation à Du Périer*, one notes the pattern of 'm' and 'p', and their contrast with the 'v' and 's' in its third line, all interspersed with liquid 'l' sounds:

> De *m*urmurer contre elle, et *p*erdre *p*atience
>   Il est *m*al à *p*ro*p*os:
> *V*ouloir *c*e que Dieu *v*eut est la *s*eule *s*cien*c*e
>   Qui nous *m*et en re*p*os.

This is enhanced by another feature for which Malherbe was celebrated in his own time, his cultivation of rich and unusual rhymes. These serve a double purpose: they mark clearly the end of the line, and thus the measure of the self-contained alexandrine, and they also add greatly to the sonority of the verse.

Malherbe thus devotes great care and artistry to the details of his verses, but each line does not, of course, stand in isolation; it can be seen from examples already quoted how even the finest lines both contribute to, and draw extra resonance from, the larger unit of the stanza. It follows, then, that Malherbe's choice of stanza forms, and his handling of them, is an extremely important element in his poetry. Much of the strength of his work derives from his skill in constructing his firm, clear, and largely self-contained stanzas. He almost never wrote in continuous alexandrine couplets, and also at a quite early date moved away from isometric quatrains (that is, with all lines of the same length) – one celebrated work in alexandrine quatrains, the *Dessein de quitter une dame* (p. 6), is a very early poem, and it is significant that Malherbe never authorized its reprinting after 1607. Such forms as these are relatively undemanding technically, and are perhaps best suited to a different type of poetry, in which the sense of tight formal discipline is not so important; it is interesting, for example, to compare Malherbe's practice with Théophile's use of isometric quatrains in *Le Matin* and *La Solitude*, and of alexandrine couplets in poems such as the *Satire première* and his *Elégies*. In contrast, Malherbe constantly explored the resources of new combinations of metre and rhyme, and the variety of stanza-forms in his work is extraordinary. René Fromilhague has calculated that in his ninety-two poems in stanzas he uses no fewer than forty-seven different forms, or an average of fewer than two poems in each form. In each poem, one can study the effects gained through its particular stanza-form. In the *Prière pour le Roi Henri le Grand*, for example, the movement of the poem is slow and dignified, as befits its subject. This is achieved through Malherbe's use of the six-line stanza, or *sizain*, entirely in alexandrines. The long lines themselves are very frequently end-stopped, and often have a strongly marked caesura, less to point an antithesis in this poem than to amplify a concept through its reformulation (e.g. lines 67-68); while the great majority of the *sizains* have a pause in the sense after the third line. This slows up the movement of the stanza, and leads to a typical structure, particularly through the middle part of the long poem, where an idea is formulated in the first three lines, then illustrated or restated in the next three; or, alternatively, the two halves of the stanza can stand in antithesis to one another, contrasting, for example, war with peace, vice with virtue, or the past with the future (e.g. lines 55-60, 67-72, 79-84). However, there are also a number of exceptions in this poem (in later works the pattern is never varied), which prevent the rhythm from becoming too repetitive and predictable (e.g. lines 85-90), and are often used for a cumulative effect (lines 109-114).

Very frequently, Malherbe will choose a stanza which juxtaposes alexandrines with shorter lines of six syllables (i.e. exactly half the length), as in the *Consolation à Du Périer*, the two poems *Pour Alcandre*, and the late works *Pour le Roi* and *Paraphrase du Psaume CXLV*. The effects gained through these shorter lines are diverse, but the most obvious are when the poet either prolongs the rhythm through *enjambement* over a line and a half, or alternatively uses them to give prominence to an idea through its succinct expression in a phrase that contrasts with the longer lines, a brevity that is often made appropriate to the sense. Both of these can be seen, for example, in the *Consolation à Du Périer*. In this poem the alexandrines and hexasyllables alternate in quatrains, and the regularity of this alternation gives the verse a sense of measure and balance, but also allows for considerable flexibility in the rhythmic patterns created. Longer phrases can be built up (lines 61-62), or the short lines used to contrast with the longer, as in lines 15-16 already quoted; or even, as in lines 13-14, to form a balanced antithesis with the second half of the preceding alexandrine (les plus belles choses / le pire destin), whose first half had introduced the subject (le monde) of the antithesis – it being, appropriately, the second element, the 'pire destin', that is strongly emphasized through the division between the lines. The use made of the short lines in the *Paraphrase du Psaume CXLV*, too, is well worth detailed study. No two stanzas are the same in this, from the forceful repetitions of the first stanza, which act as the climax of its accumulated imperatives, to the very effective mirroring of the meaning in lines 16-18:

> Et dans ces grands tombeaux, où leurs âmes hautaines
>> Font encore les vaines,
>> Ils sont mangés des vers.

Here, the grandeur of earthly pretensions is amplified through one and a half alexandrines with a striking *enjambement*, and the final pitiless contrast with the reality of the worms is thereby made all the more stark. Some of the forms Malherbe chooses are highly unusual and demanding. The *Chanson* on pp. 15-16, for example, is in quatrains of 9, 9, 10, 10 syllables, while another *Chanson* not included here ('Chère beauté que mon âme ravie . . .') consists of seven six-line stanzas of 10, 9, 7, 10, 8, 11 syllables. It is noteworthy that these two works are called 'Chanson', and the reason for their unusual form, with the exceptional number of imparisyllabic lines, is that they were written to suit a musical setting. It has been calculated that at least twenty-one of Malherbe's lyrics were composed to fit a set tune, or were put to music afterwards, and there is no doubt that he was always acutely conscious of the close relationship between lyric poetry and its musical origins. This is, in fact, one of the reasons behind his insistence on correctness of form, since (as he himself pointed out to Racan) marked irregularities in prosody, and the lack of a uniform strophic structure, make poetry unsuitable for setting to music.

When a poet devotes great attention to the technical excellence of his work, it can occur that the actual subject-matter of his poems might seem less important than the art with which they are written. That this might be true in Malherbe's case was felt even by his contemporaries (see Guez de Balzac's comments in the passage quoted in the Appendix, p. 73), and it can cause some difficulty for the modern reader with, possibly, different expectations in poetry. We find the same typical features of theme and structure appearing in a large number of his poems, and these can perhaps best be studied in a type of verse in which he created some of his most outstanding achievements, the heroic ode on 'official' subjects. Two examples are given here, one early and one late, to show how his manner progressed.

In such a work, his task is to celebrate and immortalize some state event or undertaking of the king's; the event itself may now appear of relatively minor importance, but using it as a basis, Malherbe gives superb expression to a whole complex of attitudes towards king and state. He celebrates the achievements of the monarch and the need for firm, stable government, and constantly contrasts these with the horrors, real or threatened, of factional unrest and civil war (an all too recent memory in France). The odes usually end on a note of anticipation of future glories, and a rhetorical call for a new Crusade by a newly-united France. These poems are often called 'logical', which is a difficult word to apply to poetry; but there is undoubtedly a clear, coherent movement of ideas. In Malherbe's ideal of poetry, the parts are rigorously subordinated to the effect of the whole, and nothing should be allowed to detract from the measured harmony of the overall design. His imagery, for example, is rarely startling, original, or intellectually stimulating. In the opening of the *Prière pour le Roi Henri le Grand*, the metaphors –storms, dark nights, dangerous rocks– are wholly conventional, and are drawn from the common stock of familiar poetic imagery. This is not the place for unexpected new perceptions; for Malherbe, the stately formulation of the grand theme is far better served by the dignified use of hallowed concepts which, to the reader, would already be associated with this type of poem. On the other hand, a favourite ennobling technique of Malherbe's is that of employing abstractions, often personified, rather than more specific terms with concrete associations; and in the syntax, too, ennobling devices are used, particularly that of inversion – both in the structure of a phrase, and also the placing of a resounding adjective before a noun (e.g. *Prière*, lines 97-102). However convoluted the phrasing, though, it is always resolved by the last line of the stanza, whose power is often increased by a contrasting simplicity of statement.

In another major category of Malherbe's work, his love poetry, we find a considerable range of form and mood, as well as a distinction between personal works and those written on commission for patrons. It is, however, always characteristic. He is not concerned with the refined exploration of the nuances of the emotions, and the emotional stance of his love poetry is generally straightforward and uncomplicated (*Dessein de quitter une dame*, the *Chanson* 'Sus, debout . . .'). The commissioned pieces, of course, are written under additional constraints. For example, in *Il plaint la captivité. . .*, when he writes on behalf of the aging Henri IV in his passion for the fifteen-year-old Charlotte de Montmorency, the ideas are expressed very largely in clichés, Henri ('le grand Alcandre') being cast as it were as a star-crossed lover from a pastoral novel, with Charlotte's impending removal from Court seen in a 'songe funeste' in a series of romanesque tableaux. No doubt this was just the sort of hyperbolic fictionalized presentation of himself with which Henri could identify, and Malherbe certainly achieved a prodigious personal success with the king during this episode; but what strikes the modern reader in these poems (indeed in all Malherbe's love poems) is not the subtlety or originality of the ideas but the qualities of their presentation, the harmonic skill and rhythmic balance of the stanzas, their firmness and controlled progression – exactly the qualities, in fact, that so distinguish his state odes.

The common impression of Malherbe is that of a pedantic and dogmatic man, a sterile and impersonal poet obsessed with technique, whose chief themes are the celebration of those in power and the flawless enunciation of Stoic platitudes about life and death. The reality, though, is far more complex. It is certainly true that neo-stoic philosophy was always of great importance for him, as it was for many men in the first half of the seventeenth century; it formed a major current in contemporary thought, and was to achieve its finest literary expression in Corneille. As already mentioned, Malherbe was the admiring friend of the neo-stoic philosopher Guillaume Du Vair, and himself devoted much time to translating Seneca.

However, far from being cold and unfeeling, Malherbe was in his life an exceptionally passionate man, for whom the Stoic ideal of impassivity was probably attractive precisely because it contrasted with, and offered a counterbalance to, his own turbulent emotions. This can be clearly seen in his reaction to the death of his son Marc-Antoine in 1627, 'ce fils qui fut si brave, et que j'aimai si fort', which can be followed in his correspondence for the rest of his life, and which is so violently expressed in his explicit rejection of Stoic consolation (and Christian forgiveness) in the sonnet *Sur la mort de son fils*. Indeed, there is a curious sense of suppressed violence in much of his best poetry, clearly evident in the state poems and political pieces (*Prophétie du Dieu de Seine*, p. 17), and to be felt even in some of the love poems and psalm paraphrases. In the state as in the spirit, the longing for peace, order, and stability has a profound importance for Malherbe, and it is plain from his correspondence and many contemporary anecdotes that his admiration for Henri IV (and later Richelieu) was genuine. In this, he is expressing attitudes shared by many of his contemporaries. It is no wonder that he believed a strong central authority to be essential when one considers the experiences of his lifetime and the contemporary situation in France, after the forty years of appalling social chaos of the civil wars, with the return of anarchy constantly threatened by court intrigues, disaffected great nobles, or the well-organized Protestant minority.

The allegation of sterility against Malherbe, on the other hand, is to some extent justified. His output is surprisingly small, consisting of only about one hundred and forty poems in all, and even this number contains many disjointed fragments of works which were never completed. Numerous anecdotes circulated in his lifetime about his extreme slowness of composition; he ascribed this himself to his laziness, which he frequently comments on in his correspondence, but there is probably a good deal of truth in the view that, as he matured, his technical demands became so exacting that he found it increasingly difficult to finish off a major poem to his own satisfaction. He does often seem to have found poetic composition a considerable effort, particularly (and perhaps understandably) with commissioned pieces; however, not all his poetry was ground out like this, and he was capable of writing quickly when he felt moved to do so. The sonnet 'Beaux et grands bâtiments . . .' (pp. 14-15), one of his finest, and his own favourite, was one of two sonnets that he wrote within a day for his mistress; he sent the poems to 'Caliste' (the Vicomtesse d'Auchy) from the court at Fontainebleau in early June 1607, saying 'Je les commençai samedi au soir, et les achevai le lendemain à la même heure' – although he does jocularly attribute 'cette diligence extraordinaire' to a miracle, the day concerned being Pentecost!

There are, of course, very evident limitations to the ideal of poetry to which Malherbe devoted himself. To judge from his works, he was entirely indifferent to the beauties of nature, and one might look in vain for any strong sense of transporting inspiration, let alone the *Herzensergießungen* of the Romantics. But what he does undertake he achieves supremely well; there is in his best poetry a sense of majesty, grandeur, and strength, and a nobility and harmony of expression that, as many later poets have remarked, can be admired but can rarely be equalled.

THÉOPHILE DE VIAU

Malherbe always enjoyed immense prestige to the end of his life, but from about 1615 onwards the presence of a new school of younger poets came increasingly to be felt – a deliberately 'modern' school, who proclaimed their independence of the literature of the past, and of Malherbe himself (although profiting when they chose from both), and developed a new and very attractive type of poetry. The dominant personality of this group was undoubtedly Théophile de Viau. For a few years he achieved dazzling success, not only for his natural gifts but also for the provocative ideas he expresses and his well-attested reputation for blasphemy and moral subversiveness, all calculated to delight his admirers and outrage the orthodox; and this was followed by a dramatic eclipse that aroused equally strong emotions on all sides. Indeed, the course of his life and the circumstances of his death attained an almost symbolic significance for his admirers and enemies alike.

Théophile de Viau was born in 1590 near Clairac in Gascony, into a Protestant family belonging to the 'petite noblesse'. He received a conventional enough education, but then spent some time travelling with a troupe of wandering actors, writing plays for them. He came to find this discipline increasingly irksome, as he commented later in his *Elégie à une dame* (see Appendix, p. 74), but he was to produce one admirable 'literary' drama later in his career, in *Les Amours tragiques de Pyrame et Tisbé* (1623). In 1615 he appeared at the University of Leiden in the company of his friend and fellow-Gascon Guez de Balzac (who later turned against him in his adversity), but his real success began in Paris shortly afterwards. From about 1616 he achieved fame as a popular court poet, much patronized by young noblemen, whom he delighted by his intelligence and wit, and also by his bold and unconventional ideas. However, the court during this unsettled period could be a dangerous place for a gifted and ambitious young poet. In 1618 a promising contemporary, Etienne Durand, was burnt as a result of unwise involvement in political intrigue, and Théophile himself began to attract opposition for his over-free writing; the first effect of this was his exile from Paris for a year in 1619, the same year that the

Italian naturalist philosopher and eccentric Vanini, who strongly influenced Théophile's ideas, was burnt in Toulouse.

After his return to court in 1620 he enjoyed the period of his greatest success, both personal and literary, but before long the storm-clouds began to gather once again. Théophile became the object of the implacable hostility of the powerful and excitable Jesuit Père Garasse and his sinister colleague Père Voisin, and the pretext for their move against him came in 1621 with the publication of an anthology of erotic and obscene verse, *Le Parnasse des poètes satyriques*. The first poem was boldly entitled 'Sonnet par le sieur Théophile', and sets the tone for the whole collection with its suggestions of blasphemy, obscene subject-matter, and spectacularly bawdy language (the first line reads 'Philis, tout est foutu, je meurs de la vérole . . .'). Théophile always vehemently denied that he was the author, but the important point is that the attribution was accepted as being at the least highly plausible – that is to say, whether or not he wrote that particular sonnet, it was typical of the sort of verse that he did produce, and shows what his reputation was like. He attempted to flee to the Low Countries in 1623, but was intercepted near the frontier, arrested, and thrown into prison in the Conciergerie in extremely bad conditions. Here he remained for nearly two years, charged principally with 'lèse-majesté divine' (blasphemy and heresy). He was lucky to escape with his life, but eventually in 1625 was merely given the token sentence of ten years' banishment, never rigidly enforced. However, his health had been ruined during his years of incarceration, and after a year of freedom he died in Paris on 25 September 1626, at the age of 36.

Théophile's poetry was immensely popular both during his lifetime and throughout the seventeenth century, a point to be borne in mind when considering generalizations about the evolution of literary taste. In terms of the number of editions of his work (a good indication of what the public was actually buying and reading) he was by far the most popular poet of the century, enjoying a success unrivalled until La Fontaine: it has been calculated that there were no fewer than ninety-three editions of his work up to 1700, as opposed to just sixteen of Malherbe's, and in the period 1628-1635, immediately after Malherbe's death, the contrast is just as striking, with nineteen as opposed to five. This popularity was the subject of some indignation among the neo-classical critics of the latter part of the century, and is reflected, for example, in Boileau's incidental sneer in his Satire IX (see Appendix, p. 77).

Théophile's own poetry is very different from that of Malherbe in almost every respect, including his conception of his art. When seventeenth-century readers write of Théophile, the one quality that they praise above all is his power of imagination, which is hardly a distinguishing feature of Malherbe's work; and this basic difference of literary personality is reflected in his verse, where, as we shall see, he practises a far freer and looser form of poem than the Malherbian ideal. It is particularly interesting to note that in the opening lines of one of his Elégies ('Souverain qui régis l'influence des vers . . .') he states that:

Je me contenterais d'égaler en mon art
La douceur de Malherbe ou l'ardeur de Ronsard

– that is to say, he would aim to combine Malherbe's harmonic skill with the inspiration and imaginative force that so characterize the sixteenth-century poet. Théophile's attitude towards Malherbe was one of admiration for the older poet's achievements (particularly of the fame and position that he had attained), and a broad acceptance of his technical reforms, coupled with a refusal to be bound by any example, however prestigious. He expresses this attitude clearly in the *Elégie à une dame* (see Appendix, pp. 73-74), where he combines an appreciation of the great man's worth with a proclamation of his own independence, and of the necessity for the poet to speak with his own voice ('Malherbe a très bien fait, mais il a fait pour lui . . . J'approuve que chacun écrive à sa façon'). He ridicules the host of mediocre versifiers who copied the forms of Malherbe's verse, and even his images and rhymes, without any touch of his genius –the peacock's feathers put on by the crow– and his witty parody of the hackneyed repetition of Malherbe's famous exotic rhymes was to remain appropriate for the next thirty years and more.

Théophile's poetic output is considerable, and shows some evolution. *Le Matin* and *La Solitude* are among his earliest works, and although they have always been extremely popular, he developed away from this type of piece himself; in his unfinished fragment of prose fiction entitled *Première Journée* (usually referred to as *Fragments d'une histoire comique*) he even appears specifically to parody the opening stanzas of *Le Matin* as a type of style to be avoided (see Appendix, p. 75). In the years around 1620 he produced both his satires and much of his best love poetry, including the poems to Caliste and Cloris, which are commonly seen (on rather scanty evidence, it must be said) as representing groups of works, or even cycles, reflecting personal experiences. After the great crisis of his imprisonment his poetry tends to be strongly personal, drawing much on his sufferings, with appeals for help, polemical attacks on his persecutors, and haunting evocations of the beauties of nature beyond his cell. It is from this period, also, that dates a group of works that form one of his most impressive achievements in verse, the ten odes entitled *La Maison de Silvie* (Ode III is given complete in this anthology). These were probably begun before his arrest, and finished in prison, and they gain much of their unique quality from the circumstances in which they were written. They sing the praises of his young protectress, the duchesse de Montmorency, and her estate at Chantilly, with great charm and brilliance. The poet allows his imagination to dwell on the beauties of the park, recreating and heightening them, and elaborating the descriptions with Ovidean mythological fantasies; and at the same time there runs the theme of the poet himself and his sufferings, symbolically represented by the nightingale creating beauty from her private sorrows. In spite of this evolution in Théophile's poetry, however, many common features persist throughout, both in subject-matter and style.

A very striking element in his work is the individual outlook on life, which colours his nature poetry and love poetry, as well as the more overtly philosophical pieces such as the satires; this is the complex of attitudes usually referred to as his *libertinage*. This is not the place to go into the whole question of *libertinage* in the early seventeenth century, but some awareness of the meaning of the term is essential for understanding Théophile. The word carried suggestions of loose morals from an early date (certainly appropriate in Théophile's case), but also at this time was used to denote a particular philosophic attitude. There is no doubt that for much of his career Théophile was far from a devout Christian. He had long since abandoned the Protestantism of his upbringing (although retaining the Reformed Church's scepticism as regards many of the devotional practices and superstitious accretions of Catholicism), and his final evolution to an apparently sincere Catholicism dates only from the last years of his life. So far as one can judge, his philosophical ideas were not simply a posture of revolt, but derive from a far wider movement whose origins are complex, being shaped in part by the social and political background of the previous century, and influenced both by Montaigne and, perhaps most strongly, by ideas generated and debated in sixteenth-century Italy. The *libertin* looks for inspiration and guidance not to God and the Church, but to Nature – a Nature governed ultimately by an unalterable Destiny, and seen as a liberating force, far superior to the dogmas of revealed religion (particularly the unpredictable, jealous, and vengeful God of the Old Testament), or any imposed moral restraint. The world follows its regular course, free from arbitrary divine intervention; man is seen as just another type of animal among the rest, and should act accordingly. As a general principle, one's natural instincts and desires are thus the true guide to happiness; to gratify them is the wise course, and to repress or denounce them is unnatural, and therefore wrong.

It was clearly highly dangerous to express such ideas in print, and the fate of Vanini, who expounded many of them in his *De arcanis naturae*, served as an eloquent warning. Théophile was, on the whole, fairly cautious in this respect. One can, however, discern a distinctly cavalier attitude to, for example, the Church's moral teaching and the sacrament of confession in witty love-poems like the two sonnets on pp. 34-35; and he goes furthest in expounding his philosophy in his *Satire première* (pp. 35-38), which contains some lines of remarkable boldness. Man does not possess a 'divine essence' (lines 5-10), he is comparable, but inferior, to the beasts of the field who are free from such perversions of natural instincts as a sense of evil, guilt, the fear of death, or any hope of immortality (lines 19-42); the poet attacks the inconstancy of man and all forms of moral restriction, all rendered futile by the finality of death, and proclaims his ideal of following one's natural instincts – 'J'approuve qu'un chacun suive en tout la nature' (lines 83-90, 92-102).

Such an attitude is clearly intimately bound up with Théophile's passion for natural beauty –all beauty, whether a landscape or a woman– and his exquisite appreciation of all forms of sensual gratification. He expresses this passion in a most attractive passage in his *Première Journée*, which is given here in the Appendix, p. 75. Thus it is that his nature-poetry and his love-poetry are closely linked; it is quite typical that the two early poems, *Le Matin* and *La Solitude*, should begin as nature poems and end as love poems. In the *Elégies* too, when a poem describes the poet's love for a girl, he pictures them together amid the beauties of nature (e.g. *Elégie*, pp. 44-47, lines 116-21); and when tiring of her it is in terms of a preference for the natural world that he conveys his changing mood (*Elégie*, pp. 39-41, lines 63-70).

Théophile's *libertinage* thus has a profound influence on his sensuality. In order to appreciate this unusual love-poetry fully, one needs to be aware of some of the traditional conventions of the genre up to this time – a large element in Théophile's effectiveness consists in his reversal of the expected commonplaces, or parody of the language and attitudes that had become so closely associated with love-poetry that any sense of unpredictability or individual poetic personality was in danger of being lost. The established conventions, dominated by the example of Petrarch, present love as a spiritual experience, if at times a harrowing one. The lover professes absolute faithfulness, even when without hope of a reward, and is content to worship from afar; in his lady's presence he is a model of discretion and decorum, often professing himself overcome with timidity at her beauty. Far from demanding a physical reward for his love, it is reward enough in itself; and his lady's coldness and rebuffs serve only to intensify his passion. Such attitudes are expressed in equally stereotyped forms: the ordered sonnet-cycle and familiar imagery that had been exhaustively exploited in the previous century, and in which the aesthetic pleasure for the reader resides, not in any new insights into the emotions, but in the poet's skilful reworking of conventional themes.

Much of Théophile's best love-poetry can be seen as a direct reaction against such predictable traditions. He frequently insists that he will not profess his devotion to a pure lady on a pedestal, and ridicules those who do (e.g. *Elégie*, pp. 40-41, lines 71-80; *Elégie*, p. 45, lines 18-31). On the contrary, he demands reciprocity in love: 'Je ne saurais aimer si je ne vois qu'on m'aime'; this theme, that true enjoyment is mutual enjoyment, recurs often in his work, and is developed in particular throughout the *Elégie* on pp. 44-47. Equally, he has no intention of swearing eternal constancy, since that would be foreign to his natural instincts. If the lady affects coldness in the approved literary manner, far from this increasing his passion, he will merely abandon such a fruitless and one-sided pursuit, and turn to other pleasures instead (e.g. *Ode*, pp. 41-44). He describes the moods of melancholy mixed in with his love, whether tiring of the girl, or falling into a rêverie on human mortality as he looks at her pretty young face (*Elégie*, pp. 39-41); all our life is bounded by the ultimate decay and the silence of the tomb, and for this very reason we must enjoy our pleasures while we can: to deny pleasure is to deny life.

It is this that gives its particular force to an outstanding poem, *A Monsieur de L., sur la mort de son père* (pp. 48-50), which is worth considering briefly as an example of the success that can be obtained through Théophile's technique, and also an expression of some of his most characteristic ideas. In this, the first four stanzas establish a relationship between poetic creation, the beauties of nature, and the fact of death and the poet's reaction to it, all linked through Théophile's symbolic use of fire, light, and the sun (for life, joy, natural beauty, and inspiration) and cold and darkness (winter, sterility, and death). The first part of the poem reaches a climax at the beginning of stanza four, which also introduces the themes that follow. Now the subject of the poem moves definitively to death, apparently the ultimate 'outrage' to everything that nature stands for. The following three stanzas present the universality and finality of death; while thereafter the perspective of the poem broadens to a cosmic scale, with the themes of the end of the world and the return to primaeval chaos. The poet rejects the myths of the ancients (and by implication the claims of astrology and possibly religion), then evokes, with an ever increasing scale, the end of all things and the dissolution of the whole of nature, the entire picture being given a startling immediacy by the final two lines of the poem. On this disquieting note –so different from the resignation of Malherbe's *Consolation à Du Périer*– the work ends. However, these final five stanzas cast a new light on the attitude to death adopted in the first seven stanzas. Death is only apparently an 'outrage', an alien intrusion into the joys of life; the true message of the work is that, on the contrary, death is a necessary part of the workings of nature, and is to be accepted as such; and the impermanence, instability, and unpredictability of all things serve to heighten our awareness of life and its precious moments.

Such ideas clearly demand an equally distinctive form of expression. Théophile quite deliberately rejects Malherbe's rigorous insistence on correctness of form in favour of a far freer type of poem, full of movement in time or place, or in the development of a sequence of ideas. This does not, of course, represent spontaneous composition (although the poet might well successfully attempt to suggest this), but a high degree of considered art. He returns on many occasions to the justification of this type of work. The *Elégie à une dame* shows that he is perfectly well aware of what he is doing in differing from the expected pattern of a poem's structure, in order to achieve his ideal of 'des vers qui ne soient pas contraints'; as he writes,

> Je ne veux point unir le fil de mon sujet;
> Diversement je laisse et reprends mon objet . . .
> La règle me déplaît; j'écris confusément:
> Jamais un bon esprit ne fait rien qu'aisément.

Equally, in the *Première Journée* he concludes an exposition of his artistic beliefs with the revealing comment: 'Or ces digressions me plaisent, je me laisse aller à ma fantaisie, et quelque pensée qui se présente, je n'en détourne point la plume'.

Thus the form that he adopts serves as an excellent medium for the personal and familiar tone of his verse. His nature poetry, for example, is a good illustration of how, where Malherbe's inevitable tendency is to universalize, Théophile is concerned to particularize. Nature rarely appears in Malherbe save in the most imprecise and conventional form, to be used for its symbolic value rather than as a subject for picturesque description, whereas Théophile will characteristically describe a series of precise and evocative little scenes. His technique in his nature poetry has been called 'description by vignette'; and the individual 'vignettes' are often brilliantly successful, highly coloured by the poet's imaginative vision, a mixture of precise detail and deliberately artificial conceits, so that there is a constant delicate interplay between fantasy and reality. Some recent critics have made a determined effort to argue for a thematic unity in these poems, even in *La Solitude*, which probably forms an amalgam of three shorter early 'odelettes' put together at a later date; but there is no doubt that Théophile does not attempt to achieve the Malherbian sense of firm structural control.

The same is true of many of Théophile's love poems, which can be a good deal more complex than Malherbe's, or indeed most of his predecessors. He will often encompass great variety of mood within a single poem, growing colder or more passionate as his verse progresses, or even digressing on to a different subject altogether – 'Dès le commencement j'ai changé de sujet', as he observes at the end of one *Elégie* (p. 41). His treatment of the familiar clichés of love poetry is equally complex, both parodying and taking seriously the attitudes of the passionate lover of literary tradition, and adopting a poetic persona (which may or may not, of course, coincide with the poet's own emotions) which itself can be highly subtle and paradoxical, and contributes greatly to the fascination of this poetry. Many of his later poems are unquestionably strongly personal, with their references to his sufferings, appeals for help, and abuse of his enemies, and it is always true that the poet's persona, the 'je' in the poems, plays a quite exceptionally important role in his work. A statistical survey has shown that Théophile uses the first person singular in his poetry far more frequently than any of the other contemporary poets studied, including Saint-Amant [Jean Marmier, 'La poésie de Théophile de Viau, théâtre du moi', *Papers in French Seventeenth-Century Literature*, no. 9 (Summer, 1978), 50-65]. However, exactly what one is to make of this aspect of his love poetry is something of an open question. His concern to appear spontaneous and colloquial (reinforced by his frequent choice of the light octosyllabic metre) has caused many critics to read these poems as autobiographical statements; but one should also bear in mind the element of deliberate paradox in this, and perhaps see in them rather the effect of Théophile's concern to renew and transform the conventions of love poetry by handling the subject in an unexpected way.

Enough contrasts have already been made between Théophile and Malherbe for it to be clear that the technique of the two poets differs in almost every important respect, and we have also noted how Théophile employs verse-forms such as isometric quatrains, and long poems in alexandrine couplets, which are almost never used by Malherbe. The effect of these, and also his handling of his octosyllabic stanzas, is to give his work a relative simplicity and flexibility of form, with a good deal of freedom in the movement of the poem, rather than a sense of order and formal mastery almost as an end in itself. His alexandrines, also, are generally much more flexible, as suits the subject-matter; he does not aspire to the measured symmetries, antitheses, and amplifications of the Malherbian alexandrine, but instead aims for more fluid rhythms to suit the discursive and personal tone of his poetry.

Later in the seventeenth century, many of the features that particularly distinguish Théophile's poetry came to be seen as defects from the point of view of classical regularity and correctness. The modern reader, however, is liable to be far more receptive to Théophile's own view of his art, and indeed to find in his work some of the most immediately attractive poetry of the century.

SAINT-AMANT

Among Théophile's young friends were several who themselves proceeded to distinguished literary careers, and one of the most gifted, and most unusual, was Saint-Amant. He was born in Rouen in 1594, into a fairly prosperous Protestant merchant family; he was actually baptized Antoine Girard, but during the course of his career progressively ennobled his name to the much more impressive Marc-Antoine de Gérard, sieur de Saint-Amant. His family had a close connection with the sea, and, although his youth is poorly documented, it certainly included extensive voyages after his period of study. Their details are somewhat obscure, but he did visit the Canaries, parts of West Africa, and parts of America, including the Caribbean; most probably, he accompanied one or more of the trading voyages which followed this common triangular pattern. His love of travel remained a remarkable feature through all his life, and the extent of his lifetime's peregrinations is considerable by any standards.

Saint-Amant arrived in Paris around 1619, having already written some poetry. He mixed easily in a variety of different circles, including the *libertin* milieu associated with Théophile, and rapidly established himself as a popular figure with his wit and good cheer, and also his skill on the lute, an accomplishment for which he was famous. He is found as one of the drinking companions of the Comte d'Harcourt, and the Duc de Retz, in particular, was an early patron and friend; Saint-Amant wrote many of his poems of the 1620s while staying on Retz's estates in Brittany and on Belle-Ile, off the Breton coast. During the course of his career he attached himself to a series of patrons, and many of his voyages are the result of his accompanying them on military or diplomatic missions.

One cannot hope to follow Saint-Amant in all his travels, since many of the details remain unclear, and much distorted by legend. However, a brief survey of the most important of them will give some idea of his activity. He was at the siege of La Rochelle in 1628 and possibly, though not certainly, crossed the Alps to Piedmont in 1629, and made a voyage to Morocco (or, according to some biographers, to the West Indies) in the same year. In 1631 he visited England, and in 1633-34 accompanied Créqui on his ambassadorial visit to Rome. He was in Paris in 1634, at the centre of the literary life of the capital, and was a founder-member of the Académie Française in that year. In 1636-37 he took part in the naval expedition mounted by Harcourt against the Iles de Lérins, which had been seized by the Spanish; he sailed from the Ile de Ré, passed through the Straits of Gibraltar, and visited Parma and Sardinia before taking part in the successful assault on the islands; and in 1640 he is apparently briefly to be found commanding a small ship on surveillance operations off Corsica (this admittedly sounds implausible, but the documents studied by Jean Lagny (*Le Poète Saint-Amant*, pp. 254-56) appear unequivocal). He spent 1643-44 in England with Harcourt's mission, and in 1647 spent some time staying at Collioure, on the Mediterranean coast. Saint-Amant's current protectress, Marie de Gonzague, had married the king of Poland, and in

1649 he undertook the last great journey of his life, travelling to Warsaw by way of Flanders (where he was briefly imprisoned by the Spaniards), Amsterdam, and North Germany. He moved on to Sweden in 1650, where he was well received by Queen Christina, before returning to France in 1651. He spent the remaining years of his life in Paris, Le Mans, or Rouen, and died in Paris in 1661, having to some extent survived both his fame and his fortune.

Saint-Amant's character was as singular as his life. He has in the past been popularly portrayed as a sort of literary Falstaff, fat, hearty, and ignorant, as in Boileau's picture of 'tel autrefois qu'on vit . . . Charbonner de ses vers les murs d'un cabaret' (see Appendix, p. 78). To a large extent this image is the result of deliberate self-caricature by the poet; he goes out of his way to comment on his lack of learning (e.g. at the end of *La Solitude*) –usually in order to stress the correspondingly powerful role of inspiration in his poetry– and presents himself to the world as 'le bon gros Saint-Amant' (*Le Melon*), an amiable idler (*La Pipe*, *Le Paresseux*), or, in another mood, the roistering toper of the burlesque poems (*L'Enamouré*). However, this is far from the whole man. He had a lively intelligence, and a wide-ranging curiosity in intellectual matters; when in Italy, he frequented Campanella in Rome and had long conversations with Galileo in Siena, and he went out of his way when travelling to Warsaw to visit Copernicus's tomb in Torun. His protestations of ignorance are not to be taken seriously. He was perhaps not outstandingly learned by contemporary standards, and he had no love for pedantry or displays of erudition for its own sake, but he was clearly well read in the standard Latin classics at the very least, just like every other educated man of his time. Ovid, in particular, seems to have been a favourite poet of his, and a work such as *La Solitude* is full of Ovidean echoes, both direct references to episodes from the *Metamorphoses*, and many half-submerged or even unconscious reminiscences; often, for example, what appears to be a description of a personally observed natural scene turns out to be a transposition of a passage in the Latin poet. Furthermore, he was very widely read in modern languages – Spanish, some English, and above all Italian. As we shall see, his humorous pieces owe much to the burlesque and mock-epic poets of the sixteenth and early seventeenth centuries such as Berni and Tassoni; while another particularly important influence is the work of Giambattista Marino, who lived in Paris from 1615 to 1623. Marino's brilliant and fascinating poetry has as its aim to 'far stupir', to astonish and delight the reader by its protean invention and dazzling *concetti*; Saint-Amant's enthusiasm for the Italian poet was celebrated among his contemporaries, and the effect of this can be clearly perceived in his own work. One also finds reflected his love of music, and above all of the visual arts, which he saw as having a close relationship with poetry (he greatly admired Poussin, whose acquaintance he probably made while in Italy); and, as with Théophile, he displays a most attractive sensitivity to the beauty of nature. There is, in short, a serious side to Saint-Amant which, while it only infrequently dominates the mood of a whole poem, is nevertheless to be felt in much that he wrote. Thus he sought to guarantee his immortality with a biblical epic, *Moïse sauvé* (which he oddly termed an 'Idylle héroïque'); although it is very uneven, and indeed for long was remembered only because of Boileau's mockery of it (see Appendix, p. 78), it shows considerable erudition, and contains much fine and even noble verse. Finally, a unique ingredient in his work is the experience of his travels, which contributes a wide and sometimes exotic range of subject-matter, imagery, and reference.

Saint-Amant is totally un-'classical'. Like Théophile, he respected and admired Malherbe (as is shown, for example, at the end of *Le Melon*), but his own practice of his art is utterly different. To the strong elements of humour and bizarrerie in his work is added a highly-developed aesthetic sensitivity, and a serious awareness of the type of poetry that he is consciously trying to write. Most importantly, in the maturity of the middle phase of his career (c. 1632-50) he did elaborate a coherent poetic theory, which is centred on a type of poem that he derived from the sixteenth-century Italian poets, the *caprice*. The principal general feature of the Italian *capriccio* is its flexibility; it is a self-consciously 'modern' form which deliberately breaks literary conventions, particularly the distinction between different genres and tones within one work, and is susceptible to a high degree of personal interpretation by the various poets that essayed it. The most famous early exponent of the *capriccio* (from c. 1530) was Francesco Berni, who wrote satires based on paradox, with low subject-matter and a familiar and dramatic tone in the verse; this genre then developed in several different directions, but generally away from the cruder forms of realism towards an emphasis on the exuberant handling of language, and was given a new lease of life by Marino, who used it as an excuse for a prodigious display of his imaginative and above all linguistic resources.

It is this curious genre that Saint-Amant attempts to renew in French, adapting and transforming the Italian models in his own highly individual way. The freedom of composition that this gives him –freedom not only from literary 'rules', but also from the reader's expectation of the poem– enables him to write unified works deliberately based on a principle of diversity and contrast. He will often change direction in a poem, or even the metre (as in *Le Melon*), and unexpectedly vary the tone from the noble to the familiar, or the mythological to the realistic; and everything is heightened by his astonishing linguistic virtuosity. The richness of his vocabulary is indeed unique, and makes a major contribution to the vigour and originality of his verse. The most important statement of his aims is found in his Preface to *Le Passage de Gibraltar* of 1640, which is given in the Appendix. This text is crucial for understanding Saint-Amant's intentions: he spells out his belief that 'le principal but de la poésie doit être de plaire', the importance of diversity and variety within a work, and above all that the poet must be 'maître absolu de la langue'.

Although these principles seem to have been formalized only in his middle period, Saint-Amant was clearly working them out from an early date, and elements of them are found throughout his work. An important early statement of them is found in the penultimate stanza of *La Solitude* (lines 181-90), where he explains his design in writing 'cette poésie Pleine de licence et d'ardeur', emphasizing his 'fantaisie' and his 'liberté', and demonstrating all the variety that one work can encompass ('Tantôt chagrin, tantôt joyeux . . .'). One is inevitably reminded of Théophile's practice, and particularly his *Elégie à une dame*; Saint-Amant expressed the same attitude in a similar poem from a rather later date, *Le Contemplateur*:

> Voilà comme, selon l'objet,
> Mon esprit changeant de projet
> Saute de pensée en pensée.
> La diversité plaît aux yeux. . .

Thus his poems are full of movement, in time as well as in place. A work such as *La Solitude* is remarkable for the number of transition words such as 'Là . . . là', 'tantôt . . . tantôt', 'quelquefois', and 'lors', giving to the descriptions a constant sense of variety and novelty, as the sea, for example, changes from violent storm to flat calm. This passage also shows how Saint-Amant will mix different moods in close juxtaposition, when, in the account of objects washed up after the storm, we move from the serious (corpses, ships) to the grotesque (sea-monsters), to the *précieux* (diamonds, ambergris), followed in the very next stanza by an example of the love of the mystery and *trompe-l'œil* of reflections in water that fascinated many poets of this period.

This same poem well illustrates another notable feature of Saint-Amant, his strongly visual imagination. He has a love of pictorial detail and a gift for exact observation of the normally trivial (as he wrote in the introduction to *Moïse sauvé*, 'la description des moindres choses est de mon apanage particulier'), and at the same time a predilection for original and outlandish material. Thus in lines 48-60 we have the unexpectedly precise detail of the frogs, the waterfowl preening itself, and another pair mating —where he cannot resist a passing *concetto* on the fire of love and the watery element— shortly followed by four stanzas of description of ruins, witches, and ghosts, that mark a distinct change of atmosphere in the poem. The work is indeed, as he says (lines 173-74), a 'fantasque tableau Fait d'une peinture vivante' – highly pictural, startlingly 'fantasque', but above all, 'vivante'. The weakest part of his output, on the other hand, is to be found in his encomiastic verse, where his task is simply to flatter the great, or sing the praises of a patron; he rarely seems able to carry this through successfully, and all too often he loses himself in banality or hyperingenious metaphorical elaborations.

One can see the strengths and weaknesses of Saint-Amant's work in a passage such as the famous description of the Israelites crossing the Red Sea in *Moïse sauvé* (pp. 62-63), which was created by the poet on the basis of the barest of indications in the biblical narrative. We find here the poet's love of picturesque detail, with the fantastic imaginings and dazzling colours of the vision of the newly-exposed sea-bed, his repeated use of paradox and antithesis as he exploits every aspect of the extraordinary scene, and the unpredictable way in which he allows his imagination to create a living panorama for the reader, full of movement and wonder. A typical touch is that he portrays the Red Sea as being really red, 'de liquides rubis'. He explained why he adopted this fiction in a letter to a learned correspondent, Samuel Bochart: 'J'ai feint la mer Erythrée de couleur rouge, selon la créance vulgaire . . . parce que la chose est plus rare, et que cela me fournissait d'une plus belle matière d'écrire'; in other words, what he considers to be the exotic beauty of an idea is justification in itself, without regard to mundane literality. There are many fine and skilful lines which show his mastery of rhythm and harmony in his verse: the heavy and slow beat of the camels in line 17, 'Là des chameaux chargés la troupe lente et forte', and the similar effect of the alliteration in line 23; the leaping movement of the horse contrasted with the ponderous vowels of the whale in lines 21-22; and the light, irregular rhythms (including *enjambements*) that so delightfully convey the picture of the little child trotting around happily picking up pretty pebbles (lines 25-32); and yet, for all this, one might well feel some force in Boileau's objection that Saint-Amant shows a basic lack of the sustained high seriousness required for a successful epic poem. In a lighter vein, on the other hand, he is inimitable, and a poem such as *Le Melon* is a masterpiece of its kind.

These three authors follow one another in approximate chronological sequence, and it is possible to trace a kind of evolution from Malherbe to Théophile and then Saint-Amant in their exploration of new forms of poetic expression. Nevertheless, it was the Malherbian ideal, however modified, that was to be most admired as the century progressed, as Boileau's comments illustrate, and the other poets suffered from being judged by standards that were not their own. It was not really until the present century that Théophile and Saint-Amant came to be read once more with full critical understanding, and both have seen a considerable renewal of popularity; indeed, many modern readers find their verse more immediately sympathetic than the disciplined art of Malherbe. Yet any such critical preconditions are unnecessarily limiting to the enjoyment of poetry. Each of the three can be appreciated for his own unique qualities, since each particularly excels at a quite different type of poetry; it is their very diversity that helps to make their study so rewarding.

NOTE ON THE TEXTS

Since this selection is intended as a straightforward introduction to the
three poets, spelling and punctuation have been modernized throughout,
except in a few cases where this would distort the scansion or seriously
affect the rhyme. Explanatory notes have been kept to a minimum; how-
ever, classical references which might be unfamiliar to a modern reader
have been elucidated. A number of useful ancillary passages have been
collected together as an Appendix. The Select Bibliography indicates the
principal contemporary and modern editions of the poets' work, together
with a selection of anthologies for further reading among other poets of
the period, and a few important critical works.

MALHERBE, THÉOPHILE DE VIAU
AND SAINT-AMANT

MALHERBE

CONSOLATION A MONSIEUR DU PERIER, GENTILHOMME
D'AIX-EN-PROVENCE, SUR LA MORT DE SA FILLE

Ta douleur, du Périer, sera donc éternelle,
   Et les tristes discours
Que te met en esprit l'amitié paternelle
   L'augmenteront toujours?

5   Le malheur de ta fille, au tombeau descendue
     Par un commun trépas,
Est-ce quelque Dédale, où ta raison perdue
     Ne se retrouve pas?

Je sais de quels appas son enfance était pleine
10   Et n'ai pas entrepris,
Injurieux ami, de soulager ta peine
     Avecque son mépris.

Mais elle était du monde, où les plus belles choses
     Ont le pire destin,
15   Et rose elle a vécu ce que vivent les roses,
     L'espace d'un matin.

Puis quand ainsi serait, que selon ta prière
     Elle aurait obtenu
D'avoir en cheveux blancs terminé sa carrière,
20   Qu'en fût-il advenu?

Penses-tu que, plus vieille, en la maison céleste
    Elle eût eu plus d'accueil?
Ou qu'elle eût moins senti la poussière funeste
    Et les vers du cercueil?

25 Non, non, mon du Périer, aussitôt que la Parque
    Ote l'âme du corps,
L'âge s'évanouit au deçà de la barque
    Et ne suit point les morts.

Tithon n'a plus les ans qui le firent cigale,
30   Et Pluton aujourd'hui,
Sans égard du passé, les mérites égale
    D'Archémore et de lui.

Ne te lasse donc plus d'inutiles complaintes,
    Mais, sage à l'avenir,
35 Aime une ombre comme ombre, et de cendres éteintes
    Eteins le souvenir.

C'est bien, je le confesse, une juste coutume
    Que le cœur affligé,
Par le canal des yeux vidant son amertume,
40   Cherche d'être allégé.

Même quand il advient que la tombe sépare
    Ce que Nature a joint,
Celui qui ne s'émeut a l'âme d'un barbare,
    Ou n'en a du tout point.

45 Mais d'être inconsolable, et dedans sa mémoire
    Enfermer un ennui,
N'est-ce pas se haïr pour acquérir la gloire
    De bien aimer autrui?

Priam, qui vit ses fils abattus par Achille,
50   Dénué de support,
Et hors de tout espoir du salut de sa ville,
      Reçut du réconfort.

François, quand la Castille, inégale à ses armes,
      Lui vola son Dauphin,
55 Sembla d'un si grand coup devoir jeter des larmes
      Qui n'eussent point de fin.

Il les sécha pourtant, et, comme un autre Alcide,
      Contre fortune instruit,
Fit qu'à ses ennemis d'un acte si perfide
60   La honte fut le fruit.

Leur camp, qui la Durance avait presque tarie
      De bataillons épais,
Entendant sa constance, eut peur de sa furie,
      Et demanda la paix.

65 De moi déjà deux fois d'une pareille foudre
      Je me suis vu perclus,
Et deux fois la raison m'a si bien fait résoudre,
      Qu'il ne m'en souvient plus.

Non qu'il ne me soit grief que la tombe possède
70   Ce qui me fut si cher,
Mais en un accident qui n'a point de remède
      Il n'en faut point chercher.

La mort a des rigueurs à nulle autre pareilles;
      On a beau la prier,
75 La cruelle qu'elle est se bouche les oreilles
      Et nous laisse crier.

Le pauvre en sa cabane, où le chaume le couvre,
    Est sujet à ses lois:
Et la garde qui veille aux barrières du Louvre
80   N'en défend point nos rois.

De murmurer contr'elle et perdre patience,
    Il est mal à propos:
Vouloir ce que Dieu veut est la seule science
    Qui nous met en repos.

DESSEIN DE QUITTER UNE DAME
QUI NE LE CONTENTAIT QUE DE PROMESSES

Beauté, mon beau souci, de qui l'âme incertaine
A, comme l'Océan, son flux et son reflux,
Pensez de vous résoudre à soulager ma peine,
Ou je me vais résoudre à ne la souffrir plus.

5   Vos yeux ont des appas que j'aime et que je prise,
Et qui peuvent beacoup dessus ma liberté,
Mais pour me retenir, s'ils font cas de la prise,
Il leur faut de l'amour autant que de beauté.

Quand je pense être au point que cela s'accomplisse,
10   Quelque excuse toujours en empêche l'effet:
C'est la toile sans fin de la femme d'Ulysse,
Dont l'ouvrage du soir au matin se défait.

Madame, avisez-y, vous perdez votre gloire
De me l'avoir promis, et vous rire de moi;
15   S'il ne vous en souvient, vous manquez de mémoire,
Et s'il vous en souvient, vous n'avez point de foi.

J'avais toujours fait compte, aimant chose si haute,
De ne m'en séparer qu'avecque le trépas;
S'il arrive autrement, ce sera votre faute,
20   De faire des serments et ne les tenir pas.

PRIERE POUR LE ROI HENRI LE GRAND ALLANT EN LIMOUSIN

O Dieu, dont les bontés de nos larmes touchées
Ont aux vaines fureurs les armes arrachées,
Et rangé l'insolence aux pieds de la raison,
Puisqu'à rien d'imparfait ta louange n'aspire,
5   Achève ton ouvrage au bien de cet empire,
Et nous rends l'embonpoint comme la guérison.

Nous sommes sous un Roi si vaillant et si sage,
Et qui si dignement a fait l'apprentissage
De toutes les vertus propres à commander,
10   Qu'il semble que cet heur nous impose silence,
Et qu'assurés par lui de toute violence,
Nous n'avons plus sujet de te rien demander.

Certes quiconque a vu pleuvoir dessus nos têtes
Les funestes éclats des plus grandes tempêtes
15   Qu'excitèrent jamais deux contraires partis,
Et n'en voit aujourd'hui nulle marque paraître,
En ce miracle seul il peut assez connaître
Quelle force a la main qui nous a garantis.

Mais quoi! De quelque soin qu'incessamment il veille,
20   Quelque gloire qu'il ait à nulle autre pareille,
Et quelque excès d'amour qu'il porte à notre bien,
Comme échapperons-nous, en des nuits si profondes,
Parmi tant de rochers que lui cachent les ondes,
Si ton entendement ne gouverne le sien?

25   Un malheur inconnu glisse parmi les hommes,
Qui les rend ennemis du repos où nous sommes:
La plupart de leurs vœux tendent au changement;
Et, comme s'ils vivaient des misères publiques,
Pour les renouveler ils font tant de pratiques
30   Que qui n'a point de peur n'a point de jugement.

En ce fâcheux état, ce qui nous réconforte,
C'est que la bonne cause est toujours la plus forte,
Et qu'un bras si puissant t'ayant pour son appui,
Quand la rébellion, plus qu'une hydre féconde,
35 Aurait pour le combattre assemblé tout le monde,
Tout le monde assemblé s'enfuirait devant lui.

Conforme donc, Seigneur, ta grâce à nos pensées;
Ote-nous ces objets qui des choses passées
Ramènent à nos yeux le triste souvenir;
40 Et, comme sa valeur, maîtresse de l'orage,
A nous donner la paix a montré son courage,
Fais luire sa prudence à nous l'entretenir.

Il n'a point son espoir au nombre des armées,
Etant bien assuré que ces vaines fumées
45 N'ajoutent que de l'ombre à nos obscurités.
L'aide qu'il veut avoir, c'est que tu le conseilles:
Si tu le fais, Seigneur, il fera des merveilles,
Et vaincra nos souhaits par nos prospérités.

Les fuites des méchants, tant soient-elles secrètes,
50 Quand il les poursuivra, n'auront point de cachettes;
Aux lieux les plus profonds ils seront éclairés;
Il verra sans effet leur honte se produire,
Et rendra les desseins qu'ils feront pour lui nuire
Aussitôt confondus comme délibérés.

55 La rigueur de ses lois, après tant de licence,
Redonnera le cœur à la faible innocence,
Que dedans la misère on faisait envieillir;
A ceux qui l'oppressaient il ôtera l'audace;
Et, sans distinction de richesse ou de race,
60 Tous, de peur de la peine, auront peur de faillir.

La terreur de son nom rendra nos villes fortes;
On n'en gardera plus ni les murs ni les portes,
Les veilles cesseront aux sommets de nos tours;
Le fer, mieux employé, cultivera la terre,
65 Et le peuple, qui tremble aux frayeurs de la guerre,
Si ce n'est pour danser, n'aura plus de tambours.

Loin des mœurs de son siècle il bannira les vices,
L'oisive nonchalance et les molles délices,
Qui nous avaient portés jusqu'aux derniers hasards;
70   Les vertus reviendront de palmes couronnées,
Et ses justes faveurs, aux mérites données,
Feront ressusciter l'excellence des arts.

La foi de ses aïeux, ton amour et ta crainte,
Dont il porte dans l'âme une éternelle empreinte,
75   D'actes de piété ne pourront l'assouvir;
Il étendra ta gloire autant que sa puissance,
Et n'ayant rien si cher que ton obéissance,
Où tu le fais régner, il te fera servir.

Tu nous rendras alors nos douces destinées;
80   Nous ne reverrons plus ces fâcheuses années
Qui pour les plus heureux n'ont produit que des pleurs;
Toute sorte de biens comblera nos familles,
La moisson de nos champs lassera les faucilles,
Et les fruits passeront la promesse des fleurs.

85   La fin de tant d'ennuis dont nous fûmes la proie
Nous ravira les sens de merveille et de joie;
Et, d'autant que le monde est ainsi composé
Qu'une bonne fortune en craint une mauvaise,
Ton pouvoir absolu, pour conserver notre aise,
90   Conservera celui qui nous l'aura causé.

Quand un roi fainéant, la vergogne des princes,
Laissant à ses flatteurs le soin de ses provinces,
Entre les voluptés indignement s'endort,
Quoique l'on dissimule, on n'en fait point d'estime;
95   Et, si la vérité se peut dire sans crime,
C'est avecque plaisir qu'on survit à sa mort.

Mais ce Roi des bons rois l'éternel exemplaire,
Qui de notre salut est l'ange tutélaire,
L'infaillible refuge et l'assuré secours,
100   Son extrême douceur, ayant dompté l'envie,
De quels jours assez longs peut-il borner sa vie,
Que notre affection ne les juge trop courts?

Nous voyons les esprits nés à la tyrannie,
Ennuyés de couver leur cruelle manie,
105   Tourner tous leurs conseils à notre affliction:
Et lisons clairement dedans leur conscience
Que, s'ils tiennent la bride à leur impatience,
Nous n'en sommes tenus qu'à sa protection.

Qu'il vive donc, Seigneur, et qu'il nous fasse vivre!
110   Que de toutes ces peurs nos âmes il délivre;
Et, rendant l'univers de son heur étonné,
Ajoute chaque jour quelque nouvelle marque
Au nom, qu'il s'est acquis, du plus rare monarque
Que ta bonté propice ait jamais couronné!

115   Cependant son Dauphin, d'une vitesse prompte,
Des ans de sa jeunesse accomplira le compte,
Et, suivant de l'honneur les aimable appas,
Des faits si renommés ourdira son histoire
Que ceux qui, dedans l'ombre éternellement noire,
120   Ignorent le soleil ne l'ignoreront pas.

Par sa fatale main, qui vengera nos pertes,
L'Espagne pleurera ses provinces désertes,
Ses châteaux abattus et ses champs déconfits;
Et si de nos discords l'infâme vitupère
125   A pu la dérober aux victoires du père,
Nous la verrons captive aux victoires du fils.

POUR ALCANDRE
AU RETOUR D'ORANTHE A FONTAINEBLEAU

Revenez, mes plaisirs, ma dame est revenue,
Et les vœux que j'ai faits pour revoir ses beaux yeux,
Rendant par les soupirs ma douleur reconnue,
    Ont eu grâce des cieux.

5   Les voici de retour, ces astres adorables,
Où prend mon océan son flux et son reflux;
Soucis, retirez-vous, cherchez les misérables:
    Je ne vous connais plus!

Peut-on voir ce miracle, où le soin de nature
10   A semé comme fleurs tant d'aimables appas,
Et ne confesser point qu'il n'est pire aventure
    Que de ne la voir pas?

Certes l'autre soleil d'une erreur vagabonde
Court inutilement par ses douze maisons:
15   C'est elle, et non pas lui, qui fait sentir au monde
    Le change des saisons.

Avecque sa beauté toutes beautés arrivent;
Ces déserts sont jardins de l'un à l'autre bout,
Tant l'extrême pouvoir des grâces qui la suivent
20   Les pénètre partout.

Ces bois en ont repris leur verdure nouvelle,
L'orage en est cessé, l'air en est éclairci,
Et même ces canaux ont leur course plus belle
    Depuis qu'elle est ici.

25   De moi, que les respects obligent au silence,
J'ai beau me contrefaire, et beau dissimuler:
Les douceurs où je nage ont une violence
    Qui ne se peut celer.

Mais, ô rigueur du sort! tandis que je m'arrête
30   A chatouiller mon âme en ce contentement,
Je ne m'aperçois pas que le destin m'apprête
    Un autre partement.

Arrière ces pensers que la crainte m'envoie!
Je ne sais que trop bien l'inconstance du sort;
35   Mais de m'ôter le goût d'une si chère joie
    C'est me donner la mort.

IL PLAINT LA CAPTIVITE DE SA MAITRESSE
Pour Alcandre
STANCES

Que d'épines, amour, accompagnent tes roses!
Que d'un aveugle erreur tu laisses toutes choses
    A la merci du sort!
Qu'en tes prospérités à bon droit on soupire!
5   Et qu'il est malaisé de vivre en ton empire
    Sans désirer la mort!

Je sers, je le confesse, une jeune merveille,
En rares qualités, à nulle autre pareille,
    Seule semblable à soi:
10   Et, sans faire le vain, mon aventure est telle,
Que de la même ardeur que je brûle pour elle
    Elle brûle pour moi.

Mais parmi tout cet heur, ô dure destinée!
Que de tragiques soins, comme oiseaux de Phinée
15   Sens-je me dévorer:
Et ce que je supporte avecque patience,
Ai-je quelque ennemi, s'il n'est sans conscience,
    Qui le vît sans pleurer?

La mer a moins de vents qui ses vagues irritent,
20   Que je n'ai de pensers qui tous me sollicitent,
      D'un funeste dessein:
Je ne trouve la paix qu'à me faire la guerre:
Et si l'Enfer est fable au centre de la terre,
      Il est vrai dans mon sein.

25   Depuis que le Soleil est dessus l'hémisphère,
    Qu'il monte, ou qu'il descende, il ne me voit rien faire
      Que plaindre et soupirer:
Des autres actions j'ai perdu la coutume,
Et ce qui s'offre à moi, s'il n'a de l'amertume,
30   Je ne puis l'endurer.

Comme la nuit arrive, et que par le silence,
Qui fait des bruits du jour cesser la violence,
      L'esprit est relâché:
Je vois de tous côtés sur la terre, et sur l'onde,
35   Les pavots qu'elle sème assoupir tout le monde,
      Et n'en suis point touché.

S'il m'avient quelquefois de clore les paupières,
Aussitôt ma douleur en nouvelles matières
      Fait de nouveaux efforts:
40   Et de quelque souci qu'en veillant je me ronge,
Il ne me trouble point comme le meilleur songe
      Que je fais quand je dors.

Tantôt cette beauté, dont ma flamme est le crime,
M'apparaît à l'autel, où comme une victime
45   On la veut égorger:
Tantôt je me la vois d'un pirate ravie:
Et tantôt la fortune abandonne sa vie,
      A quelque autre danger.

En ces extrémités la pauvrette s'écrie,
50   Alcandre, mon Alcandre, ôte-moi, je te prie,
      Du malheur où je suis:
La fureur me saisit, je mets la main aux armes:
Mais son destin m'arrête, et lui donner des larmes,
      C'est tout ce que je puis.

55 Voilà comme je vis, voilà ce que j'endure,
Pour une affection que je veux qui me dure
   Au-delà du trépas:
Tout ce qui me la blâme offense mon oreille:
Et qui veut m'affliger il faut qu'il me conseille
60   De ne m'affliger pas.

On me dit qu'à la fin toute chose se change:
Et qu'avecque le temps les beaux yeux de mon ange
   Reviendront m'éclairer:
Mais voyant tous les jours ses chaînes se restreindre,
65 Désolé que je suis! que ne dois-je point craindre:
   Ou que puis-je espérer?

Non, non, je veux mourir: la raison m'y convie:
Aussi bien le sujet, qui m'en donne l'envie,
   Ne peut être plus beau.
70 Et le sort qui détruit tout ce que je consulte,
Me fait voir assez clair que jamais ce tumulte
   N'aura paix qu'au tombeau.

Ainsi le grand Alcandre aux campagnes de Seine
Faisait, loin de témoins, le récit de sa peine,
75   Et se fondait en pleurs:
Le fleuve en fut ému: ses Nymphes se cachèrent:
Et l'herbe du rivage, où ses larmes touchèrent,
   Perdit toutes ses fleurs.

CHANSON (SONNET)

Beaux et grands bâtiments d'éternelle structure,
Superbes de matière et d'ouvrages divers,
Où le plus digne Roi qui soit en l'univers
Aux miracles de l'art fait céder la nature;

5   Beau parc et beaux jardins, qui dans votre clôture
Avez toujours des fleurs et des ombrages verts,
Non sans quelque démon qui défend aux hivers
D'en effacer jamais l'agréable peinture;

Lieux qui donnez aux cœurs tant d'aimables désirs,
10   Bois, fontaines, canaux, si parmi vos plaisirs
Mon humeur est chagrine et mon visage triste,

Ce n'est point qu'en effet vous n'ayez des appas;
Mais quoi que vous ayez, vous n'avez point Caliste,
Et moi je ne vois rien, quand je ne la vois pas.

CHANSON

Sus, debout, la merveille des belles!
Allons voir sur les herbes nouvelles
Luire un émail, dont la vive peinture
Défend à l'art d'imiter la nature.

5   L'air est plein d'une haleine de roses,
Tous les vents tiennent leurs bouches closes,
Et le soleil semble sortir de l'onde
Pour quelque amour plus que pour luire au monde.

On dirait, à lui voir sur la tête
10   Ses rayons comme un chapeau de fête,
Qu'il s'en va suivre en si belle journée
Encore un coup la fille de Pénée.

Toute chose aux délices conspire,
Mettez-vous en votre humeur de rire;
15   Les soins profonds d'où les rides nous viennent
A d'autres ans qu'aux vôtres appartiennent.

Il fait chaud; mais un feuillage sombre
Loin du bruit nous fournira quelque ombre,
Où nous ferons parmi les violettes
20   Mépris de l'ambre et de ses cassolettes.

Près de nous, sur les branches voisines
Des genêts, des houx, et des épines,
Le rossignol, déployant ses merveilles,
Jusqu'aux rochers donnera des oreilles.

25   Et peut-être à travers des fougères
Verrons-nous de bergers à bergères
Sein contre sein, et bouche contre bouche,
Naître et finir quelque douce escarmouche.

C'est chez eux qu'Amour est à son aise:
30   Il y saute, il y danse, il y baise,
Et foule aux pieds les contraintes serviles
De tant de lois qui le gênent aux villes.

O qu'un jour mon âme aurait de gloire
D'obtenir cette heureuse victoire,
35   Si la pitié de mes peines passées
Vous disposait à semblables pensées!

Votre honneur, le plus vain des idoles,
Vous remplit de mensonges frivoles:
Mais quel esprit que la raison conseille,
40   S'il est aimé, ne rend point de pareille?

EPIGRAMME

Cet absinthe au nez de barbet,
En ce tombeau fait sa demeure;
Chacun en rit, et moi j'en pleure,
Je le voulais voir au gibet.

EPIGRAMME

Au-dedans ce n'est qu'artifice
Ce n'est qu'artifice au-dehors
Otez-lui le fard et le vice
Vous lui ôtez l'âme et le corps.

PROPHETIE DU DIEU DE SEINE

Va-t'en à la malheure, excrément de la terre,
Monstre qui dans la paix fais les maux de la guerre,
   Et dont l'orgueil ne connaît point de lois;
En quelque haut dessein que ton esprit s'égare,
5   Tes jours sont à leur fin, ta chute se prépare,
   Regarde-moi pour la dernière fois.

C'est assez que cinq ans ton audace effrontée,
Sur des ailes de cire aux étoiles montée,
   Princes et rois ait osé défier;
10   La fortune t'appelle au rang de ses victimes
Et le ciel accusé de supporter tes crimes,
   Est résolu de se justifier.

AU ROI

Qu'avec une valeur à nulle autre seconde,
Et qui seule est fatale à notre guérison,
Votre courage mûr en sa verte saison
Nous ait acquis la paix sur la terre et sur l'onde;

5   Que l'hydre de la France, en révoltes féconde,
Par vous soit du tout morte, ou n'ait plus de poison,
Certes c'est un bonheur dont la juste raison
Promet à votre front la couronne du monde.

Mais qu'en de si beaux faits vous m'ayez pour témoin,
10   Connaissez-le, mon Roi, c'est le comble du soin
Que de vous obliger ont eu les destinées.

Tous vous savent louer, mais non également;
Les ouvrages communs vivent quelques années:
Ce que Malherbe écrit dure éternellement.

POUR LE ROI
allant châtier la rébellion des Rochellois, et chasser les Anglais, qui
faveur étaient descendus en l'île de Ré

Donc un nouveau labeur à tes armes s'apprête:
Prends ta foudre, Louis, et va comme un lion
Donner le dernier coup à la dernière tête
    De la rébellion.

5   Fais choir en sacrifice au démon de la France
Les fronts trop élevés de ces âmes d'enfer:
Et n'épargne contr'eux pour notre délivrance
    Ni le feu ni le fer.

Assez de leurs complots l'infidèle malice
10   A nourri le désordre et la sédition.
Quitte le nom de Juste, ou fais voir ta justice
    En leur punition.

Le centième décembre a les plaines ternies,
Et le centième avril les a peintes de fleurs,
15   Depuis que parmi nous leurs brutales manies
    Ne causent que des pleurs.

Dans toutes les fureurs des siècles de tes pères
Les monstres les plus noirs firent-ils jamais rien
Que l'inhumanité de ces cœurs de vipères
20   Ne renouvelle au tien?

Par qui sont aujourd'hui tant de villes désertes?
Tant de grands bâtiments en masures changés?
Et de tant de chardons les campagnes couvertes
   Que par ces enragés?

25   Les sceptres devant eux n'ont point de privilèges;
Les immortels eux-même en sont persécutés;
Et c'est aux plus saints lieux que leurs mains sacrilèges
   Font plus d'impiétés.

Marche, va les détruire: éteins-en la semence;
30   Et suis jusqu'à leur fin ton courroux généreux,
Sans jamais écouter ni pitié ni clémence
   Qui te parle pour eux.

Ils ont beau vers le ciel leurs murailles accroître;
Beau d'un soin assidu travailler à leurs forts,
35   Et creuser leurs fossés jusqu'à faire paroître
   Le jour entre les morts.

Laisse-les espérer, laisse-les entreprendre:
Il suffit que ta cause est la cause de Dieu,
Et qu'avecque ton bras elle a pour la défendre
40   Les soins de Richelieu:

Richelieu, ce prélat, de qui toute l'envie
Est de voir ta grandeur aux Indes se borner;
Et qui visiblement ne fait cas de sa vie
   Que pour te la donner.

45   Rien que ton intérêt n'occupe sa pensée;
Nuls divertissements ne l'appellent ailleurs;
Et de quelques bons yeux qu'on ait vanté Lyncée,
   Il en a de meilleurs.

Son âme toute grande est une âme hardie,
50 Qui pratique si bien l'art de nous secourir,
Que, pourvu qu'il soit cru, nous n'avons maladie
    Qu'il ne sache guérir.

Le ciel qui doit le bien selon qu'on le mérite,
Si de ce grand oracle il ne t'eût assisté,
55 Par un autre présent n'eût jamais été quitte
    Envers ta piété.

Va, ne diffère plus tes bonnes destinées:
Mon Apollon t'assure, et t'engage sa foi,
Qu'employant ce Tiphys, Syrtes et Cyanées
60   Seront havres pour toi.

Certes, ou je me trompe, ou déjà la Victoire,
Qui son plus grand honneur de tes palmes attend,
Est aux bords de Charente en son habit de gloire,
    Pour te rendre content.

65 Je la vois qui t'appelle, et qui semble te dire:
Roi, le plus grand des Rois, et qui m'est le plus cher,
Si tu veux que je t'aide à sauver ton Empire,
    Il est temps de marcher.

Que sa façon est brave, et sa mine assurée!
70 Qu'elle a fait richement son armure étoffer!
Et qu'il se connaît bien à la voir si parée
    Que tu vas triompher!

Telle en ce grand assaut, où des fils de la Terre
La rage ambitieuse à leur honte parut,
75 Elle sauva le Ciel, et rua le tonnerre
    Dont Briare mourut.

Déjà de tous côtés s'avançaient les approches:
Ici courait Mimas, là Typhon se battait,
Et là suait Euryte à détacher les roches
80   Qu'Encelade jetait.

A peine cette Vierge eut l'affaire embrassée,
Qu'aussitôt Jupiter en son trône remis,
Vit selon son désir la tempête cessée
      Et n'eut plus d'ennemis.

85   Ces Colosses d'orgueil furent tous mis en poudre,
Et tous couverts des monts qu'ils avaient arrachés;
Phlègre, qui les reçut, pût encore la foudre
      Dont ils furent touchés.

L'exemple de leur race à jamais abolie
90   Devait sous ta merci tes rebelles ployer;
Mais serait-ce raison qu'une même folie
      N'eût pas même loyer?

Déjà l'étonnement leur fait la couleur blême;
Et ce lâche voisin qu'ils sont allés quérir,
95   Misérable qu'il est, se condamne lui-même
      A fuïr ou mourir.

Sa faute le remord; Mégère le regarde
Et lui porte l'esprit à ce vrai sentiment,
Que d'une injuste offense il aura, quoiqu'il tarde,
100   Le juste châtiment.

Bien semble être la mer une barre assez forte
Pour nous ôter l'espoir qu'il puisse être battu;
Mais est-il rien de clos dont ne t'ouvre la porte
      Ton heur et ta vertu?

105 Neptune importuné de ses voiles infâmes,
Comme tu paraîtras au passage des flots,
Voudra que ses Tritons mettent la main aux rames
    Et soient tes matelots.

Là rendront tes guerriers tant de sortes de preuves,
110 Et d'une telle ardeur pousseront leurs efforts,
Que le sang étranger fera monter nos fleuves
    Au-dessus de leurs bords.

Par cet exploit fatal en tous lieux va renaître
La bonne opinion des courages françois;
115 Et le monde croira, s'il doit avoir un maître,
    Qu'il faut que tu le sois.

O que, pour avoir part en si belle aventure,
Je me souhaiterais la fortune d'Eson,
Qui, vieil comme je suis, revint contre Nature
120   En sa jeune saison!

De quel péril extrême est la guerre suivie,
Où je ne fisse voir que tout l'or du Levant
N'a rien que je compare aux honneurs d'une vie
    Perdue en te servant?

125 Toutes les autres morts n'ont mérite ni marque;
Celle-ci porte seule un éclat radieux
Qui fait revivre l'homme, et le met de la barque
    A la table des Dieux.

Mais quoi? tous les pensers dont les âmes bien nées
130 Excitent leur valeur, et flattent leur devoir,
Que sont-ce que regrets, quand le nombre d'années
    Leur ôte le pouvoir?

Ceux à qui la chaleur ne bout plus dans les veines,
En vain dans les combats ont des soins diligents;
135   Mars est comme l'Amour: ses travaux et ses peines
      Veulent de jeunes gens.

Je suis vaincu du temps; je cède à ses outrages:
Mon esprit seulement, exempt de sa rigueur,
A de quoi témoigner en ses derniers ouvrages
140   Sa première vigueur.

Les puissantes faveurs dont Parnasse m'honore,
Non loin de mon berceau commencèrent leur cours;
Je les possédai jeune, et les possède encore
      A la fin de mes jours.

145   Ce que j'en ai reçu, je veux te le produire:
Tu verras mon adresse; et ton front cette fois
Sera ceint de rayons qu'on ne vit jamais luire
      Sur la tête des Rois.

Soit que de tes lauriers ma lyre s'entretienne,
150   Soit que de tes bontés je la fasse parler,
Quel rival assez vain prétendra que la sienne
      Ait de quoi m'égaler?

Le fameux Amphion, dont la voix nonpareille,
Bâtissant une ville, étonna l'Univers,
155   Quelque bruit qu'il ait eu, n'a point fait de merveille
      Que ne fassent mes vers.

Par eux de tes beaux faits la terre sera pleine,
Et les peuples du Nil qui les auront ouïs,
Donneront de l'encens, comme ceux de la Seine,
160   Aux autels de Louis.

SUR LA MORT DE SON FILS
Sonnet

Que mon fils ait perdu sa dépouille mortelle,
Ce fils qui fut si brave, et que j'aimai si fort,
Je ne l'impute point à l'injure du sort,
Puisque finir à l'homme est chose naturelle.

5   Mais que de deux marauds la surprise infidèle
Ait terminé ses jours d'une tragique mort,
En cela ma douleur n'a point de réconfort,
Et tous mes sentiments sont d'accord avec elle.

O mon Dieu, mon Sauveur, puisque par la raison,
10   Le trouble de mon âme étant sans guérison,
Le vœu de la vengeance est un vœu légitime,

Fais que de ton appui je sois fortifié:
Ta justice t'en prie, et les auteurs du crime
Sont fils de ces bourreaux qui t'ont crucifié.

PARAPHRASE DU PSAUME CXLV
Lauda, anima mea, Dominum

N'espérons plus, mon âme, aux promesses du monde;
Sa lumière est un verre, et sa faveur une onde,
Que toujours quelque vent empêche de calmer;
Quittons ses vanités, lassons-nous de les suivre:
5   C'est Dieu qui nous fait vivre,
      C'est Dieu qu'il faut aimer.

En vain, pour satisfaire à nos lâches envies,
Nous passons près des rois tout le temps de nos vies,
A souffrir des mépris et ployer les genoux;
10   Ce qu'ils peuvent n'est rien: ils sont comme nous sommes
      Véritablement hommes,
      Et meurent comme nous.

Ont-ils rendu l'esprit, ce n'est plus que poussière
Que cette majesté si pompeuse et si fière
15 Dont l'éclat orgueilleux étonne l'univers,
Et dans ces grands tombeaux où leurs âmes hautaines
  Font encore les vaines,
  Ils sont mangés des vers.

  Là se perdent ces noms de maîtres de la terre,
20 D'arbitres de la paix, de foudres de la guerre:
Comme ils n'ont plus de sceptre ils n'ont plus de flatteurs,
Et tombent avec eux d'une chute commune
  Tous ceux que leur fortune
  Faisait leurs serviteurs.

THEOPHILE DE VIAU

LE MATIN
ODE

> L'aurore, sur le front du jour,
> Sème l'azur, l'or et l'ivoire,
> Et le soleil, lassé de boire,
> Commence son oblique tour.

5 Ses chevaux, au sortir de l'onde,
> De flamme et de clarté couverts,
> La bouche et les naseaux ouverts,
> Ronflent la lumière du monde.

> La lune fuit devant nos yeux;
10 La nuit a retiré ses voiles;
> Peu à peu le front des étoiles
> S'unit à la couleur des cieux.

> Déjà la diligente avette
> Boit la marjolaine et le thym,
15 Et revient riche du butin
> Qu'elle a pris sur le mont Hymette.

> Je vois le généreux lion
> Qui sort de sa demeure creuse,
> Hérissant sa perruque affreuse
20 Qui fait fuir Endymion.

Sa dame, entrant dans les bocages,
Compte les sangliers qu'elle a pris,
Ou dévale chez les esprits
Errant aux sombres marécages.

25   Je vois les agneaux bondissants
Sur ces blés qui ne font que naître;
Cloris, chantant, les mène paître,
Parmi ces coteaux verdissants.

Les oiseaux, d'un joyeux ramage,
30   En chantant semblent adorer
La lumière qui vient dorer
Leur cabinet et leur plumage.

La charrue écorche la plaine;
Le bouvier, qui suit les sillons,
35   Presse de voix et d'aiguillons
Le couple de bœufs qui l'entraîne.

Alix apprête son fuseau;
Sa mère, qui lui fait la tâche,
Presse le chanvre qu'elle attache
40   A sa quenouille de roseau.

Une confuse violence
Trouble le calme de la nuit,
Et la lumière, avec le bruit,
Dissipe l'ombre et le silence.

45   Alidor cherche à son réveil
L'ombre d'Iris qu'il a baisée,
Et pleure en son âme abusée
La fuite d'un si doux sommeil.

        Les bêtes sont dans leur tanière,
50   Qui tremblent de voir le soleil.
     L'homme, remis par le sommeil,
     Reprend son œuvre coutumière.

        Le forgeron est au fourneau;
     Ois comme le charbon s'allume!
55   Le fer rouge, dessus l'enclume,
     Etincelle sous le marteau.

        Cette chandelle semble morte,
     Le jour la fait évanouir;
     Le soleil vient nous éblouir;
60   Vois qu'il passe au travers la porte!

        Il est jour: levons-nous, Philis;
     Allons à notre jardinage,
     Voir s'il est, comme ton visage,
     Semé de roses et de lys.

LA SOLITUDE
ODE

        Dans ce val solitaire et sombre
     Le cerf qui brame au bruit de l'eau
     Penchant ses yeux dans un ruisseau,
     S'amuse à regarder son ombre.

5   De cette source une Naïade
     Tous les soirs ouvre le portal
     De sa demeure de cristal
     Et nous chante une sérénade.

        Les Nymphes, que la chasse attire
10   A l'ombrage de ces forêts,
     Cherchent les cabinets secrets
     Loin de l'embûche du Satyre.

    Jadis, au pied de ce grand chêne,
    Presque aussi vieux que le soleil,
15 Bacchus, l'Amour et le Sommeil
    Firent la fosse de Silène.

    Un froid et ténébreux silence
    Dort à l'ombre de ces ormeaux,
    Et les vents battent les rameaux
20 D'une amoureuse violence.

    L'esprit plus retenu s'engage
    Au plaisir de ce doux séjour,
    Où Philomèle nuit et jour
    Renouvelle un piteux langage.

25 L'orfraie et le hibou s'y perche;
    Ici vivent les loups-garous;
    Jamais la justice en courroux
    Ici de criminels ne cherche.

    Ici l'amour fait ses études;
30 Vénus y dresse des autels,
    Et les visites des mortels
    Ne troublent point ces solitudes.

    Cette forêt n'est point profane;
    Ce ne fut point sans la fâcher
35 Qu'Amour y vint jadis cacher
    Le berger qu'enseignait Diane.

    Amour pouvait par innocence
    Comme enfant, tendre ici des rêts,
    Et, comme reine des forêts,
40 Diane avait cette licence.

> Cupidon, d'une douce flamme
> Ouvrant la nuit de ce vallon,
> Mit devant les yeux d'Apollon
> Le garçon dont il avait l'âme.

45   A l'ombrage de ce bois sombre
> Hyacinthe se retira,
> Et depuis le Soleil jura
> Qu'il serait ennemi de l'ombre.

> Tout auprès le jaloux Borée,
50   Pressé d'un amoureux tourment,
> Fut la mort de ce jeune amant,
> Encore par lui soupirée.

> Sainte forêt, ma confidente,
> Je jure par le Dieu du jour,
55   Que je n'aurai jamais d'amour
> Qui ne te soit toute évidente.

> Mon ange ira par cet ombrage;
> Le soleil, le voyant venir,
> Ressentira du souvenir
60   L'accès de sa première rage.

> Corine, je te prie, approche;
> Couchons-nous sur ce tapis vert,
> Et pour être mieux à couvert,
> Entrons au creux de cette roche.

65   Ouvre tes yeux, je te supplie;
> Mille amours logent là-dedans,
> Et de leurs petits traits ardents
> Ta prunelle est toute remplie.

> Amour de tes regards soupire
70   Et, ton esclave devenu,
> Se voit lui-même retenu
> Dans les liens de ton empire.

30

O beauté sans doute immortelle,
Où les dieux trouvent des appas!
75 Par vos yeux je ne croyais pas
Que vous fussiez du tout si belle.

Qui voudrait faire une peinture
Qui peut ses traits représenter,
Il faudrait bien mieux inventer
80 Que ne fera jamais nature.

Tout un siècle les destinées
Travaillèrent après ses yeux,
Et je crois que pour faire mieux
Le temps n'a point assez d'années.

85 D'une fierté pleine d'amorce,
Ce beau visage a des regards
Qui jettent des feux et des dards
Dont les dieux aimeraient la force.

Que ton teint est de bonne grâce!
90 Qu'il est blanc et qu'il est vermeil!
Il est plus net que le soleil,
Et plus uni que de la glace.

Mon Dieu! que tes cheveux me plaisent!
Ils s'ébattent dessus ton front,
95 Et, les voyant beaux comme ils sont,
Je suis jaloux quand ils te baisent.

Belle bouche d'ambre et de rose,
Ton entretien est déplaisant
Si tu ne dis, en me baisant,
100 Qu'aimer est une belle chose.

D'un air plein d'amoureuse flamme,
Aux accents de ta douce voix,
Je vois les fleuves et les bois
S'embraser comme a fait mon âme.

105   Si tu mouilles tes doigts d'ivoire
Dans le cristal de ce ruisseau,
Le dieu qui loge dans cette eau
Aimera, s'il en ose boire.

Présente-lui ta face nue,
110 Tes yeux avecque l'eau riront,
Et dans ce miroir écriront
Que Vénus est ici venue.

Si bien elle y sera dépeinte
Que les faunes s'enflammeront,
115 Et de tes yeux qu'ils aimeront,
Ne sauront découvrir la feinte.

Entends ce dieu qui te convie
A passer dans son élément;
Ois qu'il soupire bellement
120 Sa liberté déjà ravie.

Trouble-lui cette fantaisie
Détourne-toi de ce miroir,
Tu le mettras au désespoir
Et m'ôteras la jalousie.

125   Vois-tu ce tronc et cette pierre?
Je crois qu'ils prennent garde à nous.
Et mon amour devient jaloux
De ce myrte et de ce lierre.

Sus, ma Corine! que je cueille
130 Tes baisers du matin au soir!
Vois, comment pour nous faire asseoir,
Ce myrte a laissé choir sa feuille!

Ois le pinson et la linotte,
Sur la branche de ce rosier;
135 Vois branler leur petit gosier,
Ois comme ils ont changé de note!

Approche, approche, ma Dryade!
Ici murmureront les eaux;
Ici les amoureux oiseaux
140 Chanteront une sérénade.

Prête-moi ton sein pour y boire
Des odeurs qui m'embaumeront;
Ainsi mes sens se pâmeront
Dans les lacs de tes bras d'ivoire.

145 Je baignerai mes mains folâtres
Dans les ondes de tes cheveux,
Et ta beauté prendra les vœux
De mes œillades idolâtres.

Ne crains rien, Cupidon nous garde.
150 Mon petit ange, es-tu pas mien?
Ah! je vois que tu m'aimes bien:
Tu rougis quand je te regarde.

Dieux! que cette façon timide
Est puissante sur mes esprits!
155 Renaud ne fut pas mieux épris
Par les charmes de son Armide.

Ma Corine, que je t'embrasse!
Personne ne nous voit qu'Amour;
Vois que même les yeux du jour
160 Ne trouvent ici point de place.

Les vents qui ne se peuvent taire,
Ne peuvent écouter aussi,
Et ce que nous ferons ici
Leur est un inconnu mystère.

SONNET

Chère Isis, tes beautés ont troublé la nature,
Tes yeux ont mis l'Amour dans son aveuglement,
Et les Dieux occupés après toi seulement
Laissent l'état du monde errer à l'aventure.

5 Voyant dans le soleil tes regards en peinture,
Ils en sentent leur cœur touché si vivement
Que s'ils n'étaient cloués si fort au firmament,
Ils descendraient bien tôt pour voir leur créature.

Crois-moi qu'en cette humeur ils ont peu de souci
10 Ou du bien ou du mal que nous faisons ici,
Et tandis que le Ciel endure que tu m'aimes,

Tu peux bien dans mon lit impunément coucher:
Isis, que craindrais-tu, puisque les Dieux eux-mêmes
S'estimeraient heureux de te faire pécher.

SONNET

Vous me pressez à tort pour aller à Confesse,
Beauté de qui dépend et mon bien et mon mal.
Si je n'approche pas ce sacré tribunal,
Je marque mon respect plutôt que ma paresse.

5   Je ne sens point en moi de péché qui me presse;
     Je vous aime, Philis, d'un amour sans égal;
     L'amour pour le salut n'a rien qui soit fatal,
     Et le dire tout bas marquerait ma faiblesse.

     J'en parlerai partout, je le dirai tout haut;
10   Je reconnais pourtant que j'ai quelque défaut,
     Dont je n'aurai jamais aucune repentance:

     Mon crime est que j'enrage et peste en chaque lieu,
     Malgré tous mes respects et ma persévérance,
     Que vous ne voulez pas me faire offenser Dieu.

EPIGRAMME

     Enfants, buvons à qui mieux mieux
     Sans crainte de gâter nos yeux:
     Le Soleil boit le sel et l'onde
     Sans faire jamais un repas
5   Qu'il ne soit ivre, et n'est-il pas
     Le plus bel œil de tout le monde?

     Crainte de vous charger le cœur
     Du jus sacré de ma liqueur,
     Compagnons ne quittez le verre.
10   Le Soleil en fait bien autant:
     Car après qu'il a bu d'autant
     Il rend gorge au sein de la terre.

SATIRE PREMIERE

     Qui que tu sois, de grâce écoute ma satire,
     Si quelque humeur joyeuse autre part ne t'attire,
     Aime ma hardiesse, et ne t'offense point
     De mes vers, dont l'aigreur utilement te point;
5   Toi que les éléments ont fait d'air et de boue,
     Ordinaire sujet où le malheur se joue,

Sache que ton filet, que le destin ourdit,
Est de moindre importance encor qu'on ne te dit.
Pour ne le point flatter d'une divine essence,
10 Vois la condition de ta sale naissance,
Que tiré tout sanglant de ton premier séjour,
Tu vois en gémissant la lumière du jour;
Ta bouche n'est qu'aux cris et à la faim ouverte,
Ta pauvre chair naissante est toute découverte,
15 Ton esprit ignorant encor ne forme rien,
Et moins qu'un sens brutal sait le mal et le bien.
A grand peine deux ans t'enseignent un langage,
Et des pieds et des mains te font trouver usage.
Heureux au prix de toi les animaux des champs,
20 Ils sont les moins haïs comme les moins méchants.
L'oiselet de son nid à peu de temps s'échappe,
Et ne craint point les airs que de son aile il frappe:
Les poissons en naissant commencent à nager;
Et le poulet éclos chante et cherche à manger.
25 Nature, douce mère à ces brutales races,
Plus largement qu'à toi leur a donné des grâces;
Leur vie est moins sujette aux fâcheux accidents
Qui travaillent la tienne au dehors et dedans:
La bête ne sent point peste, guerre, ou famine,
30 Le remords d'un forfait en son corps ne la mine;
Elle ignore le mal pour en avoir la peur,
Ne connaît point l'effroi de l'Achéron trompeur.
Elle a la tête basse, et les yeux contre terre,
Plus près de son repos, et plus loin du tonnerre:
35 L'ombre des trépassés n'aigrit son souvenir,
On ne voit à sa mort le désespoir venir:
Elle compte sans bruit, et loin de toute envie,
Le terme dont nature a limité sa vie,
Donne la nuit paisible aux charmes du sommeil,
40 Et tous les jours s'égaye aux clartés du soleil,
Franche de passions, et de tant de traverses,
Qu'on voit au changement de nos humeurs diverses.
Ce que veut mon caprice, à ta raison déplaît;
Ce que tu trouves beau, mon œil le trouve laid:
45 Un même train de vie au plus constant n'agrée,
La profane nous fâche autant que la sacrée.
Ceux qui dans les bourbiers des vices empêchés
Ne suivent que le mal, n'aiment que les péchés,
Sont tristes bien souvent, et ne leur est possible

50   De consumer une heure en volupté paisible.
     Le plus libre du monde est esclave à son tour,
     Souvent le plus barbare est sujet à l'amour,
     Et le plus patient que le soleil éclaire
     Se trouve quelquefois emporté de colère.
55   Comme Saturne laisse et prend une saison,
     Notre esprit abandonne et reçoit la raison.
     Je ne sais quelle humeur nos volontés maîtrise,
     Et de nos passions est la certaine crise:
     Ce qui sert aujourd'hui nous doit nuire demain,
60   On ne tient le bonheur jamais que d'une main;
     Le destin inconstant sans y penser oblige,
     Et nous faisant du bruit souvent il nous afflige;
     Les riches plus contents ne se sauraient guérir
     De la crainte de perdre et du soin d'acquérir.
65   Notre désir changeant suit la course de l'âge,
     Tel est grave et pesant qui fut jadis volage,
     Et sa masse caduque, esclave du repos,
     N'aime plus qu'à rêver, hait les joyeux propos.
     Une sale vieillesse en déplaisir confite,
70   Qui toujours se chagrine, et toujours se dépite,
     Voit tout à contre-cœur, et ses membres cassés
     Se rongent de regret de ses plaisirs passés,
     Veut traîner notre enfance à la fin de la vie,
     De notre sang bouillant veut étouffer l'envie.
75   Un vieux père rêveur aux nerfs tous refroidis,
     Sans plus se souvenir quel il était jadis,
     Alors que l'impuissance éteint sa convoitise
     Veut que notre bon sens révère sa sottise,
     Que le sang généreux étouffe sa vigueur,
80   Et qu'un esprit bien né se plaise à la rigueur.
     Il nous veut attacher nos passions humaines,
     Que son malade esprit ne juge pas bien saines.
     Soit par rébellion, ou bien par une erreur,
     Ces repreneurs fâcheux me sont tous en horreur;
85   J'approuve qu'un chacun suive en tout la nature,
     Son empire est plaisant, et sa loi n'est pas dure:
     Ne suivant que son train jusqu'au dernier moment
     Mêmes dans les malheurs on passe heureusement.
     Jamais mon jugement ne trouvera blâmable
90   Celui-là qui s'attache à ce qu'il trouve aimable. . .

     Je crois que les destins ne font venir personne

En l'être des mortels qui n'ait l'âme assez bonne,
Mais on la vient corrompre, et le céleste feu
Qui luit à la raison ne nous dure que peu:
95   Car l'imitation rompt notre bonne trame,
Et toujours chez autrui fait demeurer notre âme.
Je pense que chacun aurait assez d'esprit,
Suivant le libre train que Nature prescrit.
A qui ne sait farder ni le cœur, ni la face,
100   L'impertinence même a souvent bonne grâce:
Qui suivra son génie, et gardera sa foi,
Pour vivre bienheureux, il vivra comme moi.

STANCES

Quand tu me vois baiser tes bras,
Que tu poses nus sur tes draps,
Bien plus blancs que le linge même;
Quand tu sens ma brûlante main
5   Se promener dessus ton sein,
Tu sens bien, Cloris, que je t'aime.

Comme un dévot devers les cieux,
Mes yeux tournés devers tes yeux,
A genoux auprès de ta couche,
10   Pressé de mille ardents désirs,
Je laisse, sans ouvrir ma bouche,
Avec toi dormir mes plaisirs.

Le sommeil, aise de t'avoir,
Empêche tes yeux de me voir,
15   Et te retient dans son empire
Avec si peu de liberté
Que ton esprit tout arrêté
Ne murmure ni ne respire.

La rose en rendant son odeur,
20   Le soleil donnant son ardeur,
Diane et le char qui la traîne,
Une Naïade dedans l'eau,
Et les Grâces dans un tableau,
Font plus de bruit que ton haleine.

25   Là, je soupire auprès de toi,
Et, considérant comme quoi
Ton œil si doucement repose,
Je m'écrie: O Ciel! peux-tu bien
Tirer d'une si belle chose
30   Un si cruel mal que le mien!

ELEGIE

   Cloris, lorsque je songe, en te voyant si belle,
Que ta vie est sujette à la loi naturelle,
Et qu'à la fin les traits d'un visage si beau
Avec tout leur éclat iront dans le tombeau,
5   Sans espoir que la mort nous laisse en la pensée
Aucun ressentiment de l'amitié passée,
Je suis tout rebuté de l'aise et du souci
Que nous fait le destin qui nous gouverne ici;
Et, tombant tout à coup dans la mélancolie,
10 Je commence à blâmer un peu notre folie,
Et fais vœu de bon cœur de m'arracher un jour
La chère rêverie où m'occupe l'amour.
Aussi bien faudra-t-il qu'une vieillesse infâme
Nous gêle dans le sang les mouvements de l'âme,
15 Et que l'âge, en suivant ses révolutions,
Nous ôte la lumière avec les passions.
Ainsi je me résous de songer à la vie
Tandis que la raison m'en fait venir l'envie.
Je veux prendre un objet où mon libre désir
20 Discerne la douleur d'avecque le plaisir,
Où mes sens tous entiers, sans fraude et sans contrainte,
Ne s'embarrassent plus ni d'espoir ni de crainte;
Et, de sa vaine erreur mon cœur désabusant,
Je goûterai le bien que je verrai présent.
25 Je prendrai les douceurs à quoi je suis sensible
Le plus abondamment qu'il me sera possible.
Dieu nous a tant donné de divertissements,
Nos sens trouvent en eux tant de ravissements,
Que c'est une fureur de chercher qu'en nous-même,
30 Quelqu'un que nous aimions et quelqu'un qui nous aime.
Le cœur le mieux donné tient toujours à demi;
Chacun s'aime un peu mieux toujours que son ami:

On le suit rarement dedans la sépulture,
Le droit de l'amitié cède aux lois de nature.
35   Pour moi, si je voyais, en l'humeur où je suis,
Ton âme s'envoler aux éternelles nuits,
Quoi que puisse envers moi l'usage de tes charmes,
Je m'en consolerais avec un peu de larmes.
N'attends pas que l'amour aveugle aille suivant,
40   Dans l'horreur de la nuit, des ombrès et du vent.
Ceux qui jurent avoir l'âme encore assez forte
Pour vivre dans les yeux d'une maîtresse morte,
N'ont pas pris le loisir de voir tous les efforts
Que fait la mort hideuse à consumer un corps.
45   Quand les sens pervertis sortent de leur usage,
Qu'une laideur visible efface le visage,
Que l'esprit défaillant et les membres perclus,
En se disant adieu, ne se connaissent plus,
Que dedans un moment, après la vie éteinte,
50   La face sur son cuir n'est pas seulement peinte,
Et que l'infirmité de la puante chair,
Nous fait ouvrir la terre afin de la cacher:
Il faut être animé d'une fureur bien vive,
Ayant considéré comme la mort arrive,
55   Et comme tout l'objet de notre amour périt,
Si par un tel remède une âme ne guérit.
Cloris, tu vois qu'un jour il faudra qu'il advienne
Que le destin ravisse et ta vie et la mienne;
Mais sans te voir l'esprit ni le corps dépéri,
60   Le Ciel en soit loué! Cloris, je suis guéri.
Mon âme, en me dictant les vers que je t'envoie,
Me vient de plus en plus ressusciter la joie;
Je sens que mon esprit reprend la liberté,
Que mes yeux dévoilés connaissent la clarté,
65   Que l'objet d'un beau jour, d'un pré, d'une fontaine,
De voir comme Garonne en l'Océan se traîne,
De prendre dans mon île, en ses longs promenoirs,
La paisible fraîcheur de ses ombrages noirs,
Me plaît mieux aujourd'hui que le charme inutile
70   Des attraits dont Amour te fait voir si fertile.
Languir incessamment après une beauté,
Et ne se rebuter d'aucune cruauté,
Gagner au prix du sang une faible espérance
D'un plaisir passager qui n'est qu'en apparence,
75   Se rendre l'esprit mol, le courage abattu,

Ne mettre en aucun prix l'honneur ni la vertu,
Pour conserver son mal mettre tout en usage,
Se peindre incessamment et l'âme et le visage:
Cela tient d'un esprit où le Ciel n'a point mis
80   Ce que son influence inspire à ses amis.
Pour moi que la raison éclaire en quelque sorte,
Je ne saurais porter une fureur si forte;
Et déjà tu peux voir, au train de cet écrit,
Comme la guérison avance en mon esprit.
85   Car insensiblement ma Muse un peu légère
A passé dessus toi sa plume passagère,
Et, détournant mon cœur de son premier objet,
Dès le commencement j'ai changé de sujet,
Emporté du plaisir de voir ma veine aisée
90   Sûrement aborder ma flamme rapaisée,
Et jouer à son gré sur les propos d'aimer,
Sans avoir aujourd'hui de but que de rimer,
Et sans te demander que ton bel œil éclaire
Ces vers où je n'ai pris aucun soin de te plaire.

ODE

Cloris, pour ce petit moment
D'une volupté frénétique,
Crois-tu que mon esprit se pique
De t'aimer éternellement?
5   Lorsque mes ardeurs sont passées,
La raison change mes pensées,
Et, perdant l'amoureuse erreur,
Je me trouve dans des tristesses
Qui font que tes délicatesses
10   Commencent à me faire horreur.

A voir tant fuïr ta beauté,
Je me lasse de la poursuivre,
Et me suis résolu à vivre
Avec un peu de liberté.
15   Il ne me faut qu'une disgrâce,
Qu'encore un trait de cette audace
Qui t'a fait tant manquer de foi.

Après, tiens-moi pour un infâme
Si jamais mes yeux ni mon âme
20   Songent à s'approcher de toi.

Je me trouve prêt à te voir
Avec beaucoup d'indifférence
Et te faire une révérence
Moins d'amitié que de devoir.
25   Toutes les complaisances feintes
Où tes affections mal peintes
Ont troublé mes sens hébétés,
Je les tiens pour faibles feintises,
Et n'appelle plus que sottises
30   Ce que je nommais cruautés.

Je ne veux point te décrier
Après t'avoir loué moi-même:
Ce serait tacher du blasphème
L'autel où l'on m'a vu prier.
35   T'ayant prodigué des louanges
Que je ne devais qu'à des anges,
Je ne te les veux point ravir;
Je les donne à ta tyrannie
Pour déguiser l'ignominie
40   Que j'ai soufferte à te servir.

Je ne veux point mal à propos
Mes vers ni ton honneur détruire.
Mon dessein n'est pas de te nuire;
Je ne songe qu'à mon repos.
45   Encore auras-tu cette gloire
Que si la voix de ta mémoire
Parle à quelqu'un de mes douleurs,
On dira que ma servitude
Respecta ton ingratitude
50   Jusqu'au dernier de mes malheurs.

J'ai souffert autant que j'ai pu,
Je n'ai plus de nerfs pour tes gênes,
Ni goutte de sang dans mes veines

Qui ne se brûle à petit feu.
55 Je me sens honteux de mes larmes,
Amour n'a déjà plus de charmes,
Je suis pressé de toutes parts;
Et bientôt, quoi que tu travailles,
Je m'arracherai des entrailles
60 Tout le venin de tes regards.

Sachant bien que je meurs d'amour,
Que je brûle d'impatience,
As-tu si peu de conscience
Que de m'abandonner un jour?
65 Après ton ingrate paresse,
Si tu n'as que cette caresse
Fatale à ma crédulité,
Puisses-tu périr d'un tonnerre,
Ou que le centre de la terre
70 Cache ton infidélité!

Non, je ne saurais plus souffrir
Cette liberté de ta vie;
Tout me blâme, et tout me convie
De me plaindre et de me guérir.
75 Aussi bien ta beauté se passe,
Mon amitié change de face,
L'ardeur de mes premiers plaisirs
Perd beaucoup de sa violence,
Ma raison et ta nonchalance
80 Ont presque amorti mes désirs.

Je sais bien que la vanité
Qui te fait plaire en mes supplices
Cherche encore dans tes malices
De quoi trahir ma liberté;
85 Encore tes regards perfides
Préparent à mes sens timides
L'effort de leur éclat pipeur,
Et, malgré le plus noir outrage,
S'imaginent que mon courage
90 Devant eux n'est qu'une vapeur.

Mais je fais le plus grand serment
Que peut faire une âme bouillante
De la fureur la plus sanglante
Qui peut tourmenter un amant:
95 Je jure l'air, la terre et l'onde,
Je jure tous les Dieux du monde,
Que ni force, ni trahison,
Ni m'outrager, ni me complaire,
N'empêcheront point ma colère
100 De me donner ma guérison.

Mon tourment ne t'émeut en rien;
Ta fierté rit de ma mollesse:
Je ne crois point qu'une Déesse
Eût un orgueil comme le tien.
105 C'en est fait, je sens que mon âme
Soupire sa dernière flamme;
Tous ces regards sont superflus:
Je ne vois rien, rien ne me touche,
Je suis sans oreille et sans bouche,
110 Laisse-moi, ne me parle plus.

From ELEGIE
('Souverain qui régis l'influence des vers . . .')

. . . Ton amour, ô Cloris, a changé ma nature.
L'éclat des diamants ni du plus beau métal,
Bacchus, tout dieu qu'il est, riant dans le cristal,
Au prix de tes regards n'ont point trouvé la voie
5 Qui conduit dans mon âme une parfaite joie.
Si le sort me donnait la qualité de roi,
Si les plus chers plaisirs s'adressaient tous à moi,
Si j'étais empereur de la terre et de l'onde,
Si de ma propre main j'avais bâti le monde,
10 Et, comme le soleil, de mes regards produit
Tout ce que l'univers a de fleur et de fruit,
Si cela m'arrivait, je n'aurais pas tant d'aise
Ni tant de vanité que si Cloris me baise.
Mais j'entends d'un baiser où le cœur puisse aller
15 Avec les mouvements des yeux et du parler,

Que son âme sans peine avec moi s'entretienne,
Et que sa volonté seconde un peu la mienne.
    Amants qui vous piquez vers un objet forcé,
Qui ne savez que c'est d'un baiser bien pressé.
20 Qui ne trouvez l'amour que dans la tyrannie,
Et n'aimez les faveurs qu'en tant qu'on les vous nie,
Que vous êtes heureux en vos lâches désirs,
Puisque même vos maux font naître vos plaisirs!
Pour moi, chère Cloris, je n'en suis pas de même,
25 Je ne saurais aimer si je ne vois qu'on m'aime;
Et si peu qu'on refuse à ma sainte amitié,
Je sens que mon ardeur décroît de la moitié.
J'entends que le salaire égale mon service.
Je pense qu'autrement la constance est un vice,
30 Qu'Amour hait ces esprits qui lui sont trop dévots,
Et que la patience est la vertu des sots.
Ce que je dis, Cloris, avec plus d'assurance
D'autant que je te vois flatter mon espérance,
Et que, pour nous tenir dans cet heureux lien,
35 Je vois déjà d'accord ton esprit et le mien.
Aimons-nous, je te prie, et lorsque mon visage
Te voudra rebuter, ou mon poil ou mon âge,
Regarde en mon esprit où j'ai mis ton tableau,
Lors tu verras en moi quelque chose de beau:
40 Tu te verras logée en un petit empire
Où l'esprit de l'Amour avecque moi soupire.
Il se tient glorieux de recevoir ta loi,
Et semble qu'il poursuit même dessein que moi:
Si je vais dans tes yeux, il y va prendre place;
45 Je ne vois là-dedans que ses traits et ma face,
Je doute s'il y fait ou mon bien ou mon mal,
Et ne sais plus s'il est mon maître ou mon rival.
Je connais bien l'Amour, je sais qu'il est perfide,
Et si pour le chasser je suis un peu timide:
50 Je lui ferai toujours un traitement humain
Puisque je l'ai reçu d'une si bonne main,
Puisque c'est toi, Cloris, après l'avoir fait naître,
Qui l'a mis dans mon âme où ton œil est le maître,
Où tu vis absolue en tes commandements,
55 Où ton vouloir préside à tous mes sentiments.
C'est par toi que ces vers, d'une veine animée,
S'en vont à ma faveur flatter la renommée.
Mais je dirai partout que tes seules beautés

Ont été le Démon qui me les a dictés,
60 Et tant que tes regards luiront à ma pensée,
Sans ouvrir une veine aucunement forcée
Ma muse se promet de mériter un jour
Que ses vers soient nommés les fruits de ton amour.
Autant que ton humeur aime la poésie,
65 Je te prie, ô Cloris, aide à ma frénésie:
Et puisque je m'engage à ce divin projet,
Ne te lasse jamais de me servir d'objet.
Aujourd'hui, donne-moi tes beaux cheveux à peindre,
Tu verras une plume au Pactole se teindre,
70 Et d'une lettre d'or graver selon mes vœux
Mon âme entrelacée avecque tes cheveux.
Je ne veux point laisser ma passion oisive,
Ma veine est pour Cloris et sans fonds et sans rive.
Demain je décrirai ses yeux et ce beau front,
75 Pour elle mon génie est abondant et prompt,
Et pour voir que ma veine en ce sujet tarisse,
Il faudra voir plutôt que sa beauté périsse,
Que mes yeux dans ses yeux ne trouvent plus d'amour;
C'est-à-dire, il faut voir périr l'astre du jour:
80 Car je ne pense point que ses attraits succombent
Sous l'injure des ans tant que les cieux ne tombent.
Ils se renforceront au lieu de défaillir
Comme l'or s'embellit à force de vieillir,
Et comme le soleil, à qui le vieil usage
85 N'a point ôté l'ardeur ni changé le visage.
Toutefois, il n'importe à mon contentement
Que mon Soleil éclaire, ou meure promptement,
Puisque déjà ma vie à demi consommée
Ne se peut assurer d'être longtemps aimée,
90 Que je dois défaillir à ce divin flambeau,
Et perdre avecques moi sa mémoire au tombeau.
Mais tandis que le Ciel me souffrira de vivre
Et que le trait d'Amour me daignera poursuivre,
Je me veux consommer dans ce plaisir charmant,
95 Et me résous de vivre et mourir en aimant.

Je sais bien que Cloris ne me veut pas contraindre
Au soin perpétuel de servir et de craindre,
Qu'elle a des mouvements sujets à la pitié,
Et qu'au moins sa raison songe à mon amitié.

100   Cloris, si je venais aveuglé de tes charmes,
       Le cœur tout en soupirs, et les yeux tout en larmes,
       Demander instamment un amoureux plaisir,
       Je crois que ton amour m'en laisserait choisir.
       Maintenant que le ciel dépouille les nuages,
105   Que le front du printemps menace les orages,
       Que les champs comme toi paraissent embellis
       De quantité d'œillets, de roses et de lis:
       Que tout est sur la terre et qu'une humeur féconde
       Qu'attire le soleil fait rajeunir le monde,
110   Comme si j'avais part à la faveur des cieux
       Qui redonne l'enfance à ces bocages vieux,
       Et que ce renouveau qui rend tout agréable,
       Me rendît à tes yeux plus jeune et plus aimable,
       Je te veux conjurer avec des vœux discrets,
115   De passer avec moi quelques moments secrets.
       Nous irons dans les bois sous des feuillages sombres
       Où jamais le soleil n'a su forcer les ombres,
       Personne là-dedans n'entendra nos amours:
       Car je veux que les vents respectent nos discours,
120   Et que chaque ruisseau plus vitement s'enfuie
       De devant tes regards, de peur qu'il ne t'ennuie . . .

ODE

    Un corbeau devant moi croasse;
    Une ombre offusque mes regards;
    Deux belettes et deux renards
    Traversent l'endroit où je passe;
5   Les pieds faillent à mon cheval,
    Mon laquais tombe du haut mal;
    J'entends craqueter le tonnerre;
    Un esprit se présente à moi;
    J'ois Charon qui m'appelle à soi,
10   Je vois le centre de la terre.

    Ce ruisseau remonte en sa source;
    Un bœuf gravit sur un clocher;
    Le sang coule de ce rocher;
    Un aspic s'accouple d'une ourse;

15 Sur le haut d'une vieille tour
   Un serpent déchire un vautour;
   Le feu brûle dedans la glace,
   Le soleil est devenu noir;
   Je vois la lune qui va choir;
20 Cet arbre est sorti de sa place.

A MONSIEUR DE L., SUR LA MORT DE SON PERE
ODE

   Ote-toi, laisse-moi rêver:
   Je sens un feu se soulever
   Dont mon âme est toute embrasée.
   O beaux prés, beaux rivages verts,
5 O grand flambeau de l'univers,
   Que je trouve ma veine aisée!
   Belle aurore, douce rosée,
   Que vous m'allez donner de vers!

   Le vent s'enfuit dans les ormeaux,
10 Et pressant les feuillus rameaux,
   Abat le reste de la nue;
   Iris a perdu ses couleurs;
   L'air n'a plus d'ombre ni de pleurs;
   La bergère, aux champs revenue,
15 Mouillant sa jambe toute nue,
   Foule les herbes et les fleurs.

   Ces longues pluies dont l'hiver
   Empêchait Tircis d'arriver
   Ne seront plus continuées;
20 L'orage ne fait plus de bruit;
   La clarté dissipe la nuit,
   Ses noirceurs sont diminuées;
   Le vent emporte les nuées,
   Et voilà le soleil qui luit.

25 Mon Dieu, que le soleil est beau!
   Que les froides nuits du tombeau

Font d'outrages à la nature!
La Mort, grosse de déplaisirs,
De ténèbres et de soupirs,
30   D'os, de vers et de pourriture,
Etouffe dans sa sépulture
Et nos forces et nos désirs.

Chez elle les géants sont nains;
Les Mores et les Africains
35   Sont aussi glacés que le Scythe;
Les dieux y tirent l'aviron;
César, comme le bûcheron,
Attendant que l'on ressuscite,
Tous les jours aux bords du Cocyte
40   Se trouve au lever de Charon.

Tircis, vous y viendrez un jour;
Alors les Grâces et l'Amour
Vous quitteront sur le passage,
Et dedans ces royaumes vains,
45   Effacé du rang des humains,
Sans mouvement et sans visage,
Vous ne trouverez plus l'usage
Ni de vos yeux ni de vos mains.

Votre père est enseveli,
50   Et, dans les noirs flots de l'oubli
Où la Parque l'a fait descendre,
Il ne sait rien de votre ennui,
Et, ne fût-il mort qu'aujourd'hui,
Puisqu'il n'est plus qu'os et que cendre,
55   Il est aussi mort qu'Alexandre,
Et vous touche aussi peu que lui.

Saturne n'a plus ses maisons,
Ni ses ailes ni ses saisons;
Les Destins en ont fait une ombre.
60   Ce grand Mars n'est-il pas détruit?
Ses faits ne sont qu'un peu de bruit.
Jupiter n'est plus qu'un feu sombre

Qui se cache parmi le nombre
Des petits flambeaux de la nuit.

65   Le cours des ruisselets errants,
La fière chute des torrents,
Les rivières, les eaux salées,
Perdront et bruit et mouvement:
Le soleil, insensiblement
70   Les ayant toutes avalées,
Dedans les voûtes étoilées
Transportera leur élément.

      Le sable, le poisson, les flots,
Le navire, les matelots,
75   Tritons, et Nymphes, et Neptune,
A la fin se verront perclus:
Sur leur dos ne se verra plus
Rouler le char de la Fortune,
Et l'influence de la lune
80   Abandonnera le reflus.

      Les planètes s'arrêteront,
Les éléments se mêleront
En cette admirable structure
Dont le Ciel nous laisse jouir.
85   Ce qu'on voit, ce qu'on peut ouïr,
Passera comme une peinture:
L'impuissance de la Nature
Laissera tout évanouir.

      Celui qui, formant le soleil,
90   Arracha d'un profond sommeil
L'air et le feu, la terre et l'onde,
Renversera d'un coup de main
La demeure du genre humain
Et la base où le ciel se fonde;
95   Et ce grand désordre du monde
Peut-être arrivera demain.

REQUETE DE THEOPHILE AU ROI

Au milieu de mes libertés
Dans un plein repos de ma vie
Où mes plus molles voluptés
Semblaient avoir passé l'envie,
5   D'un trait de foudre inopiné
Que jeta le Ciel mutiné
Dessus le comble de ma joie,
Mes desseins se virent trahis,
Et moi d'un même coup la proie
10   De tous ceux que j'avais haïs . . .

Sans cordon, jartières ni gants,
Au milieu de dix hallebardes
Je flattais des gueux arrogants
Qu'on m'avait ordonné pour gardes:
15   Et nonobstant chargé de fers
On m'enfonce dans les enfers
D'une profonde et noire cave,
Où l'on n'a qu'un peu d'air puant
Des vapeurs de la froide bave
20   D'un vieux mur humide et gluant.

Dedans ce commun lieu de pleurs
Où je me vis si misérable,
Les assassins et les voleurs
Avaient un trou plus favorable:
25   Tout le monde disait de moi
Que je n'avais ni foi ni loi,
Qu'on ne connaissait point de vice
Où mon âme ne s'adonnât,
Et quelque trait que j'écrivisse
30   C'était pis qu'un assassinat.

Qu'un saint homme de grand esprit,
Enfant du bienheureux Ignace,
Disait en chaise et par écrit
Que j'étais mort par contumace,
35   Que je ne m'étais absenté
Que de peur d'être exécuté

Aussi bien que mon effigie,
Que je n'étais qu'un suborneur,
Et que j'enseignais la magie
40   Dedans les cabarets d'honneur;

Qu'on avait bandé les ressorts
De la noire et forte Machine
Dont le souple et le vaste corps
Etend ses bras jusqu'à la Chine;
45   Qu'en France et parmi l'étranger
Ils avaient dequoi se venger,
Et dequoi forger une foudre,
Dont le coup me serait fatal,
En dût-il coûter plus de poudre
50   Qu'ils n'en perdirent à Vuital;

Que le gaillard Père Guerin
Qui tous les jours fait dans la chaise
Plus de leçons à Tabarin
Qu'à tous les clercs d'un diocèse,
55   Ce vieux bateleur déguisé,
Comme s'il eût bien disposé
Et terre, et Ciel à ma ruine,
Prêchait qu'à peu de jours de là
La justice humaine et divine
60   M'immolerait à Loyola;

Que par le sentiment chrétien
D'une charité volontaire,
Infinité de gens de bien
Avaient entrepris mon affaire,
65   Qu'on était si fort irrité
Qu'en dépit de la vérité,
Que Jésus Christ a tant aimée,
Pour les intérêts du clergé
On me voulait voir en fumée
70   Soudain que je serais jugé.

On emploie de par le Roi,
De la force et de l'artifice:

Comme si Lucifer pour moi
Eût entrepris sur la justice,
75   A Paris soudain que j'y fus
J'entendais par des bruits confus
Que tout était prêt pour me cuire,
Et je doutais avec raison,
Si ce peuple m'allait conduire
80   A la Grève ou dans la prison.

    Ici donc comme en un tombeau,
Troublé du péril où je rêve,
Sans compagnie et sans flambeau,
Toujours dans le discours de Grève,
85   A l'ombre d'un petit faux jour,
Qui perce un peu l'obscure tour,
Où les bourreaux vont à la quête:
Grand Roi, l'honneur de l'univers,
Je vous présente la Requête
90   De ce pauvre faiseur de vers . . .

LA MAISON DE SILVIE
ODE III

    Dans ce parc un vallon secret,
Tout voilé de ramages sombres,
Où le soleil est si discret
Qu'il n'y force jamais les ombres,
5   Presse d'un cours si diligent
Les flots de deux ruisseaux d'argent,
Et donne une fraîcheur si vive
A tous les objets d'alentour,
Que même les martyrs d'amour
10   Y trouvent leur douleur captive.

    Un étang dort là tout auprès
Où ces fontaines violentes
Courent et font du bruit exprès
Pour éveiller ses vagues lentes.
15   Lui, d'un maintien majestueux,

Reçoit l'abord impétueux
De ces Naïades vagabondes
Qui dedans ce large vaisseau
Confondent leur petit ruisseau
20   Et ne discernent plus ses ondes.

Là, Mélicerte, en un gazon,
Frais de l'étang qui l'environne,
Fait aux cygnes une maison
Qui lui sert aussi de couronne,
25   Si la vague qui bat ses bords
Jamais avecque des trésors
N'arrive à son petit empire,
Au moins les vents et les rochers
N'y font point crier les nochers
30   Dont ils ont brisé le navire.

Là les oiseaux font leurs petits,
Et n'ont jamais vu leurs couvées
Souler les sanglants appétits
Du serpent qui les a trouvées;
35   Là n'étend point ses plis mortels
Ce monstre de qui tant d'autels
Ont jadis adoré les charmes,
Et qui, d'un gosier gémissant,
Fait tomber l'âme du passant
40   Dedans l'embûche de ses larmes.

Zéphyre en chasse les chaleurs.
Rien que les cygnes n'y repaissent;
On n'y trouve rien sous les fleurs
Que la fraîcheur dont elles naissent;
45   Le gazon garde quelquefois
Le bandeau, l'arc et le carquois
De mille amours qui se dépouillent
A l'ombrage de ses roseaux,
Et dans l'humidité des eaux
50   Trempent leurs jeunes corps qui bouillent.

L'étang leur prête sa fraîcheur,
La Naïade leur verse à boire;
Toute l'eau prend de leur blancheur
L'éclat d'une couleur d'ivoire.
55 On voit là ces nageurs ardents,
Dans les ondes qu'ils vont fendants,
Faire la guerre aux Néréides,
Qui, devant leur teint mieux uni,
Cachent leur visage terni
60 Et leur front tout coupé de rides.

Or ensemble, ores dispersés,
Ils brillent dans ce crêpe sombre
Et sous les flots qu'ils ont percés
Laissent évanouir leur ombre.
65 Parfois dans une claire nuit,
Qui du feu de leurs yeux reluit
Sans aucun ombrage de nues,
Diane quitte son berger
Et s'en va là-dedans nager
70 Avecque ses étoiles nues.

Les ondes, qui leur font l'amour,
Se refrisent sur leurs épaules,
Et font danser tout à l'entour
L'ombre des roseaux et des saules.
75 Le Dieu de l'eau, tout furieux,
Haussé pour regarder leurs yeux
Et leur poil qui flotte sur l'onde,
Du premier qu'il voit approcher
Pense voir ce jeune cocher
80 Qui fit jadis brûler le monde.

Et ce pauvre amant langoureux,
Dont le feu toujours se rallume,
Et de qui les soins amoureux
Ont fait ainsi blanchir la plume,
85 Ce beau cygne à qui Phaéton
Laissa ce lamentable ton,

Témoin d'une amitié si sainte,
Sur le dos son aile élevant,
Met ses voiles blanches au vent
90   Pour chercher l'objet de sa plainte.

Ainsi, pour flatter son ennui,
Il demande au Dieu Mélicerte
Si chacun Dieu n'est pas celui
Dont il soupire tant la perte,
95   Et, contemplant de tous côtés
La semblance de leurs beautés,
Il sent renouveler sa flamme,
Errant avec des faux plaisirs
Sur les traces des vieux désirs
100   Que conserve encore son âme.

Toujours ce furieux dessein
Entretient ses blessures fraîches,
Et fait venir contre son sein
L'air brûlant et les ondes sèches.
105   Ces attraits, empreints là-dedans
Comme avec des flambeaux ardents,
Lui rendent la peau toute noire.
Ainsi, dedans comme dehors,
Il lui tient l'esprit et le corps,
110   La voix, les yeux et la mémoire.

SAINT-AMANT

LA SOLITUDE
A Alcidon

    O que j'aime la solitude!
Que ces lieux sacrés à la nuit,
Eloignés du monde et du bruit,
Plaisent à mon inquiétude!
5   Mon Dieu! que mes yeux sont contents
De voir ces bois qui se trouvèrent
A la nativité du temps,
Et que tous les siècles révèrent,
Etre encore aussi beaux et verts
10   Qu'aux premiers jours de l'univers!

    Un gai zéphire les caresse
D'un mouvement doux et flatteur.
Rien que leur extrême hauteur
Ne fait remarquer leur vieillesse.
15   Jadis Pan et ses demi-dieux
Y vinrent chercher du refuge,
Quand Jupiter ouvrit les cieux
Pour nous envoyer le déluge,
Et, se sauvant sur leurs rameaux,
20   A peine virent-ils les eaux.

    Que sur cette épine fleurie,
Dont le printemps est amoureux,
Philomèle au chant langoureux
Entretient bien ma rêverie!
25   Que je prends de plaisir à voir
Ces monts pendants en précipices,
Qui, pour les coups du désespoir
Sont aux malheureux si propices,

Quand la cruauté de leur sort
30   Les force à rechercher la mort.

Que je trouve doux le ravage
De ces fiers torrents vagabonds,
Qui se précipitent par bonds
Dans ce vallon vert et sauvage!
35   Puis, glissant sous les arbrisseaux,
Ainsi que des serpents sur l'herbe,
Se changent en plaisants ruisseaux,
Où quelque naïade superbe
Règne, comme en son lit natal,
40   Dessus un trône de cristal!

Que j'aime ce marais paisible!
Il est tout bordé d'aliziers,
D'aulnes, de saules et d'osiers,
A qui le fer n'est point nuisible.
45   Les nymphes y cherchant le frais,
S'y viennent fournir de quenouilles,
De pipeaux, de joncs et de glais;
Où l'on voit sauter les grenouilles,
Qui de frayeur s'y vont cacher
50   Sitôt qu'on veut s'en approcher.

Là, cent mille oiseaux aquatiques,
Vivent, sans craindre, en leur repos,
Le giboyeur fin et dispos,
Avec ses mortelles pratiques.
55   L'un, tout joyeux d'un si beau jour,
S'amuse à becqueter sa plume;
L'autre alentit le feu d'amour
Qui dans l'eau même se consume,
Et prennent tous innocemment
60   Leur plaisir en cet élément.

Jamais l'été ni la froidure
N'ont vu passer dessus cette eau
Nulle charrette ni bateau,
Depuis que l'un et l'autre dure;

65 Jamais voyageur altéré
   N'y fit servir sa main de tasse;
   Jamais chevreuil désespéré
   N'y finit sa vie à la chasse;
   Et jamais le traître hameçon
70 N'en fit sortir aucun poisson.

   Que j'aime à voir la décadence
   De ces vieux châteaux ruinés,
   Contre qui les ans mutinés
   Ont déployé leur insolence!
75 Des sorciers y font leur sabbat;
   Les démons follets s'y retirent,
   Qui d'un malicieux ébat
   Trompent nos sens et nous martyrent;
   Là se nichent en mille trous
80 Les couleuvres et les hibous.

   L'orfraie, avec ses cris funèbres,
   Mortels augures des destins,
   Fait rire et danser les lutins
   Dans ces lieux remplis de ténèbres.
85 Sous un chevron de bois maudit
   Y branle le squelette horrible
   D'un pauvre amant qui se pendit
   Pour une bergère insensible,
   Qui d'un seul regard de pitié
90 Ne daigna voir son amitié.

   Aussi le Ciel, juge équitable,
   Qui maintient les lois en vigueur,
   Prononça contre sa rigueur
   Une sentence épouvantable:
95 Autour de ces vieux ossements
   Son ombre, aux peines condamnée,
   Lamente en longs gémissements
   Sa malheureuse destinée,
   Ayant, pour croître son effroi,
100 Toujours son crime devant soi.

Là se trouvent sur quelques marbres
Des devises du temps passé;
Ici l'âge a presque effacé
Ces chiffres taillés sur les arbres;
105   Le plancher du lieu le plus haut
Est tombé jusque dans la cave,
Que la limace et le crapaud
Souillent de venin et de bave;
Le lierre y croît au foyer,
110   A l'ombrage d'un grand noyer.

Là-dessous s'étend une voûte
Si sombre, en un certain endroit
Que, quand Phébus y descendroit,
Je pense qu'il n'y verrait goutte;
115   Le Sommeil aux pesants sourcils,
Enchanté d'un morne silence,
Y dort, bien loin de tous soucis,
Dans les bras de la Nonchalance,
Lâchement couché sur le dos
120   Dessus des gerbes de pavots.

Au creux de cette grotte fraîche,
Où l'Amour se pourrait geler,
Echo ne cesse de brûler
Pour son amant froid et revêche.
125   Je m'y coule sans faire bruit,
Et par la céleste harmonie
D'un doux luth, aux charmes instruit,
Je flatte sa triste manie,
Faisant répéter mes accords
130   A la voix qui lui sert de corps.

Tantôt, sortant de ces ruines,
Je monte au haut de ce rocher,
Dont le sommet semble chercher
En quel lieu se font les bruines;
135   Puis je descends tout à loisir,
Sous une falaise escarpée,
D'où je regarde avec plaisir
L'onde qui l'a presque sapée

Jusqu'au siège de Palémon.
140   Fait d'éponges et de limon.

    Que c'est une chose agréable
D'être sur le bord de la mer,
Quand elle vient à se calmer
Après quelque orage effroyable!
145   Et que les chevelus Tritons,
Hauts sur les vagues secouées,
Frappent les airs d'étranges tons
Avec leurs trompes enrouées,
Dont l'éclat rend respectueux
150   Les vents les plus impétueux.

    Tantôt l'onde, brouillant l'arène,
Murmure et frémit de courroux,
Se roulant dessus les cailloux
Qu'elle apporte et qu'elle r'entraîne.
155   Tantôt, elle étale en ses bords,
Que l'ire de Neptune outrage,
Des gens noyés, des monstres morts,
Des vaisseaux brisés du naufrage,
Des diamants, de l'ambre gris,
160   Et mille autres choses de prix.

    Tantôt, la plus claire du monde,
Elle semble un miroir flottant,
Et nous représente à l'instant
Encore d'autres cieux sous l'onde.
165   Le soleil s'y fait si bien voir,
Y contemplant son beau visage,
Qu'on est quelque temps à savoir
Si c'est lui-même, ou son image,
Et d'abord il semble à nos yeux
170   Qu'il s'est laissé tomber des cieux.

    Bernières, pour qui je me vante
De ne rien faire que de beau,
Reçois ce fantasque tableau
Fait d'une peinture vivante.

175 Je ne cherche que les déserts,
Où, rêvant tout seul, je m'amuse
A des discours assez diserts
De mon génie avec la muse;
Mais mon plus aimable entretien
180 C'est le ressouvenir du tien.

Tu vois dans cette poésie,
Pleine de licence et d'ardeur,
Les beaux rayons de la splendeur
Qui m'éclaire la fantaisie:
185 Tantôt chagrin, tantôt joyeux,
Selon que la fureur m'enflamme,
Et que l'objet s'offre à mes yeux,
Les propos me naissent en l'âme.
Sans contraindre la liberté
190 Du démon qui m'a transporté.

O que j'aime la solitude!
C'est l'élément des bons esprits,
C'est par elle que j'ai compris
L'art d'Apollon sans nulle étude:
195 Je l'aime pour l'amour de toi,
Connaissant que ton humeur l'aime,
Mais quand je pense bien à moi,
Je la hais pour la raison même;
Car elle pourrait me ravir
200 L'heur de te voir, et te servir.

LE PASSAGE DE LA MER ROUGE
(from *Moïse sauvé*)

. . . Aussitôt, à marcher toute chose étant prête,
Le sacré camp déloge, et Moïse, à la tête,
S'avançant à grands pas avecque son germain
Hausse, pour frapper l'onde, et la verge et la main.
5 L'abîme, au coup donné, s'ouvre jusqu'aux entrailles;
De liquides rubis il se fait deux murailles

Dont l'espace nouveau se remplit à l'instant
Par le peuple qui suit le pilier éclatant.
D'un et d'autre côté, ravi d'aise, il se mire;
10   De ce fond découvert le sentier il admire,
Sentier que la nature a d'un soin libéral
Paré de sablon d'or et d'arbres de coral,
Qui, plantés tout de rang, forment comme une allée
Etendue au travers d'une riche vallée,
15   Et d'où l'ambre découle ainsi qu'on vit le miel
Distiller des sapins sous l'heur du jeune ciel.

    Là des chameaux chargés la troupe lente et forte
Foule plus de trésors encor qu'elle n'en porte:
On y peut en passant de perles s'enrichir,
20   Et de la pauvreté pour jamais s'affranchir;
Là le noble cheval bondit et prend haleine
Où venait de souffler une lourde baleine;
Là passent à pied les bœufs et les moutons,
Où naguère flottaient les dauphins et les thons;
25   Là, l'enfant éveillé, courant sous la licence
Que permet à son âge une libre innocence,
Va, revient, tourne, saute, et par maint cri joyeux
Témoignant le plaisir que reçoivent ses yeux,
D'un étrange caillou, qu'à ses pieds il rencontre,
30   Fait au premier venu la précieuse montre,
Ramasse une coquille, et, d'aise transporté,
La présente à sa mère avec naïveté;
Là, quelque juste effroi qui ses pas sollicite,
S'oublie à chaque objet le fidèle exercite,
35   Et là près des remparts que l'œil peut transpercer,
Les poissons ébahis le regardent passer . . .

LA PIPE

Assis sur un fagot, une pipe à la main,
Tristement accoudé contre une cheminée,
Les yeux fixés vers terre, et l'âme mutinée,
Je songe aux cruautés de mon sort inhumain.

5   L'espoir qui me remet du jour au lendemain,
Essaie à gagner temps sur ma peine obstinée,
Et, me venant promettre une autre destinée,
M'a fait monter plus haut qu'un empereur romain.

Mais à peine cette herbe est-elle mise en cendre,
10   Qu'en mon premier état il me convient descendre
Et passer mes ennuis à redire souvent:

Non, je ne trouve point beaucoup de différence
De prendre du tabac à vivre d'espérance,
Car l'un n'est que fumée, et l'autre n'est que vent.

LE PARESSEUX

Accablé de paresse et de mélancolie,
Je rêve dans un lit où je suis fagoté,
Comme un lièvre sans os qui dort dans un pâté,
Ou comme un Don Quichotte en sa morne folie.

5   Là, sans me soucier des guerres d'Italie,
Du comte Palatin, ni de sa royauté,
Je consacre un bel hymne à cette oisiveté
Où mon âme en langueur est comme ensevelie.

Je trouve ce plaisir si doux et si charmant,
10   Que je crois que les biens me viendront en dormant,
Puisque je vois déjà s'en enfler ma bedaine,

Et hais tant le travail que, les yeux entr'ouverts,
Une main hors des draps, chez Baudouin, à peine
Ai-je pu me résoudre à t'écrire ces vers.

LES GOINFRES

Coucher trois dans un drap, sans feu ni sans chandelle,
Au profond de l'hiver, dans la salle aux fagots,
Où les chats, ruminant le langage des Goths,
Nous éclairent sans cesse en roulant la prunelle;

5   Hausser notre chevet avec une escabelle,
     Etre deux ans à jeun comme les escargots,
     Rêver en grimaçant ainsi que les magots
     Qui, bâillant au soleil, se grattent sous l'aisselle;

     Mettre au lieu de bonnet la coiffe d'un chapeau,
10   Prendre pour se couvrir la frise d'un manteau
     Dont le dessus servit à nous doubler la panse;

     Puis souffrir cent brocards d'un vieux hôte irrité,
     Qui peut fournir à peine à la moindre dépense,
     C'est ce qu'engendre enfin la prodigalité.

L'ENAMOURE

     Parbleu! j'en tiens, c'est tout de bon,
     Ma libre humeur en a dans l'aile,
     Puisque je préfère au jambon
     Le visage d'une donzelle;
5   Je suis pris dans le doux lien
     De l'archerot idalien;
     Ce dieutelet, fils de Cyprine,
     Avecque son arc mi-courbé
     A féru ma rude poitrine,
10   Et m'a fait venir à jubé.

     Mon esprit a changé d'habit,
     Il n'est plus vêtu de revêche;
     Il se raffine et se fourbit
     Aux yeux de ma belle chevêche:
15   Plus aigu, plus clair et plus net
     Qu'une dague de cabinet,
     Il estocade la tristesse,
     Et la chassant d'autour de soi
     Se vante que la politesse
20   Ne marche plus qu'avecque moi.

Je me fais friser tous les jours,
On me relève la moustache,
Je n'entrecoupe mes discours
Que de rots d'ambre et de pistache;
25 J'ai fait banqueroute au petun,
L'excès de vin m'est importun,
Dix pintes par jour me suffisent,
Encore, ô falote beauté,
Dont les regards me déconfisent,
30 Est-ce pour boire à ta santé.

L'HIVER DES ALPES

Ces atomes de feu qui sur la neige brillent,
Ces étincelles d'or, d'azur et de cristal
Dont l'hiver, au soleil, d'un lustre oriental
Pare ses cheveux blancs que les vents éparpillent;

5 Ce beau coton du ciel de quoi les monts s'habillent,
Ce pavé transparent fait du second métal,
Et cet air net et sain, propre à l'esprit vital,
Sont si doux à mes yeux que d'aise ils en pétillent.

Cette saison me plaît, j'en aime la froideur;
10 Sa robe d'innocence et de pure candeur
Couvre en quelque façon les crimes de la terre.

Aussi l'Olympien la voit d'un front humain;
Sa colère l'épargne, et jamais le tonnerre
Pour désoler ses jours ne partit de sa main.

LE MELON

    Quelle odeur sens-je en cette chambre?
Quel doux parfum de musc et d'ambre
Me vient le cerveau réjouir
Et tout le cœur épanouir?
5   Ha! Bon Dieu! j'en tombe en extase:
Ces belles fleurs qui dans ce vase
·Parent le haut de ce buffet
Feraient-elles bien cet effet?
A-t-on brûlé de la pastille?
10   N'est-ce point ce vin qui pétille
Dans le cristal que l'art humain
A fait pour couronner la main,
Et d'où sort, quand on en veut boire,
Un air de framboise à la gloire
15   Du bon terroir qui l'a porté
Pour notre éternelle santé?
Non, ce n'est rien d'entre ces choses,
Mon penser, que tu me proposes.
Qu'est-ce donc? Je l'ai découvert
20   Dans ce panier rempli de vert:
C'est un MELON, où la nature,
Par une admirable structure,
A voulu graver à l'entour
Mille plaisants chiffres d'amour,
25   Pour claire marque à tout le monde
Que d'une amitié sans seconde
Elle chérit ce doux manger,
Et que d'un souci ménager,
Travaillant aux biens de la terre,
30   Dans ce beau fruit seul elle enserre
Toutes les aimables vertus
Dont les autres sont revêtus.
    Baillez-le-moi, je vous en prie,
Que j'en commette idôlatrie:
35   O! quelle odeur! qu'il est pesant!
Et qu'il me charme en le baisant!
Page, un couteau, que je l'entame;
Mais qu'auparavant on réclame,
Par des soins au devoir instruits,
40   Pomone, qui préside aux fruits,
Afin qu'au goût il se rencontre

Aussi bon qu'il a belle montre,
Et qu'on ne trouve point en lui
Les défauts des gens d'aujourd'hui.
45   Notre prière est exaucée,
Elle a reconnu ma pensée:
C'en est fait, le voilà coupé,
Et mon espoir n'est point trompé.
O dieux! que l'éclat qu'il me lance,
50   M'en confirme bien l'excellence!
Qui vit jamais un si beau teint!
D'un jaune sanguin il se peint;
Il est massif jusques au centre,
Il a peu de grains dans le ventre,
55   Et ce peu-là, je pense encor
Que ce soient autant de grains d'or;
Il est sec, son écorce est mince;
Bref, c'est un vrai manger de prince;
Mais, bien que je ne le sois pas,
60   J'en ferai pourtant un repas.
      Ha! soutenez-moi, je me pâme,
Ce morceau me chatouille l'âme;
Il rend une douce liqueur
Qui me va confire le cœur;
65   Mon appétit se rassasie
De pure et nouvelle ambroisie,
Et mes sens, par le goût séduits,
Au nombre d'un sont tous réduits.
      Non, le coco, fruit délectable,
70   Qui lui tout seul fournit la table
De tous les mets que le désir
Puisse imaginer et choisir,
Ni les baisers d'une maîtresse,
Quand elle-même nous caresse,
75   Ni ce qu'on tire des roseaux
Que Crète nourrit dans ses eaux,
Ni le cher abricot, que j'aime,
Ni la fraise avecque la crème,
Ni la manne qui vient du ciel,
80   Ni le pur aliment du miel,
Ni la poire de Tours sacrée,
Ni la verte figue sucrée,
Ni la prune au jus délicat,
Ni même le raisin muscat

85   (Parole pour moi bien étrange),
      Ne sont qu'amertume et que fange
      Au prix de ce MELON divin,
      Honneur du climat angevin. . .

      O manger précieux! délices de la bouche!
90   O doux reptile herbu, rampant sur une couche!
      O beaucoup mieux que l'or, chef-d'œuvre d'Apollon!
      O fleur de tous les fruits! O ravissant MELON!
      Les hommes de la cour seront gens de parole,
      Les bordels de Rouen seront francs de vérole,
95   Sans vermine et sans gale on verra les pédants,
      Les preneurs de petun auront de belles dents,
      Les femmes des badauds ne seront plus coquettes,
      Les corps pleins de santé se plairont aux cliquettes,
      Les amoureux transis ne seront plus jaloux,
100   Les paisibles bourgeois hanteront les filous,
      Les meilleurs cabarets deviendront solitaires,
      Les chantres du Pont-Neuf diront de hauts mystères,
      Les pauvres Quinze-Vingts vaudront trois cents argus,
      Les esprits doux du temps paraîtront fort aigus,
105   Maillet fera des vers aussi bien que Malherbe,
      Je haïrai Faret, qui se rendra superbe,
      Pour amasser des biens avare je serai,
      Pour devenir plus grand mon cœur j'abaisserai,
      Bref, ô MELON sucrin, pour t'accabler de gloire,
110   Des faveurs de Margot je perdrai la mémoire
      Avant que je t'oublie, et que ton goût charmant
      Soit biffé des cahiers du bon gros SAINT-AMANT.

APPENDIX

EXTRACTS FROM MALHERBE'S MARGINAL NOTES IN HIS COPY OF DESPORTES'S *ŒUVRES*, 1609

The points that Malherbe is criticizing can be grouped under four main categories:

The sense of the verse, the most common type of annotation. Malherbe's comments, often sarcastic or tersely disapproving ('cheville', 'sottise'), point out when the poet has thoughtlessly slipped into trite clichés (particularly the over-familiar hackneyed Petrarchan paradoxes, e.g. nos. 12, 19), and the meaning of the verse has become repetitive, clumsy, or incoherent, or would seem fatuous when spelled out in prose: nos. 1-5, 8, 12, 14, 16, 17, 18. He is particularly severe when the sense is ambiguous or incomprehensible (nos. 2, 5, 8, 16).

The correctness of the language. Malherbe's concern that poetry should be readily accessible and follow normal usage, and his general hostility to a special 'poetic' language (such as cultivated, for example, by Ronsard), is shown also in his objections to archaic locutions and insistence on grammatical correctness: nos. 13, 15, 20 (an interesting case, where he moderates his usual dogmatism to debate the acceptability of a phrase).

Technical correctness. Malherbe concentrates particularly on the quality of the rhymes, such as in objecting to the rhyme gendarmes/ armes in no. 7, unacceptable as a homophonic rhyme because the rhyming 'armes' are actually identical in both sense and grammar (gens d'armes). Also he notes accidental, and therefore sloppy, internal rhymes (nos. 11, 18).

Finally, following on from this,

The harmony of the verse. Malherbe is very meticulous about the accidental occurence of cacophonous or ridiculous juxtapositions within a line: nos. 6, 9, 10, 11.

Desportes's text is given, followed by Malherbe's comment in italics; the underlinings are Malherbe's own.

From *DIANE: Chant d'amour*

1)   Puisqu'un amour céleste est roi de ma poitrine
Pauvre royaume.

2)   En parlant de beauté, la beauté qui m'allume
Vienne seule à ce coup mon courage émouvoir
Qu'est-ce à dire: <u>la beauté qui m'allume vienne émouvoir mon courage?</u>
Puisqu'elle vous allume, que voulez-vous qu'elle fasse davantage?

3)   Aussi les déités. . .
N'ont rien qui soit égal à leur divin pouvoir
Le divin pouvoir des déités.

4)   Se ravit <u>bienheureuse</u> en voyant sa présence
Cheville.

5)   Que l'air, la terre et la belle lumière,
Mêlés confusément faisaient un pesant corps
Il ne s'exprime pas.

6)   La volupté mignarde en chantant t'environne
<u>Tan</u>, <u>ten.</u>

7)   Tu te prends, courageux, aux plus rudes gendarmes,
Et souvent au milieu des combats et des armes
Cette rime ne vaut rien.

8)   Tu bannis les frayeurs des plus lâches courages,
Rendant l'homme craintif, hautain et généreux
Il semble qu'il fasse devenir l'homme craintif et hautain, ce qui est impertinent. Il se faut autrement expliquer.

From *LIVRE II: Sonnet 7*

9)   Madame, Amour, Fortune, et tous les éléments . . .
<u>Ma</u>, <u>da</u>, <u>ma</u>, <u>mou.</u>

10)   O songe, ange divin . . .
<u>Gean</u>, <u>ge</u>.

11)   Et ne <u>sens</u> pas <u>souvent</u> ton doux <u>allègement</u>
Note - Rime au milieu.

From *LES AMOURS D'HIPPOLYTE: Elégie III*

12)   Sans yeux je vois ma perte, et sans langue je crie
Sottise imitée de Pétrarque.

13)   <u>Or'</u> je suis plein d'amour <u>et or'</u> je n'aime pas
Or' et or' est hors d'usage.

14)   Il faut, en m'efforçant, cette pointe arracher
Quel langage: <u>il faut, en m'efforçant, faire ceci ou cela!</u>

15)   J'embrase ma fureur, la pensant <u>rendre éteinte</u>
Mal, pour <u>éteindre.</u>

16)   Mais si je perds mon temps sous l'amoureuse loi
Il s'explique mal; qu'est-ce à dire: <u>perdre son temps sous une loi?</u>

17)   Et qui d'<u>ombreuse</u> nuit ne sont jamais noircis
Sottise.

18)   L'expérience apprend. En ce commencement. . .
Rime au milieu du vers.

19)   Je sais brûler de loin et geler auprès d'elle
Sottise.

20)   Chercher mon ennemie et craindre à la trouver
<u>Craindre à trouver</u> est une phrase dont je ferais scrupule; je dirais: <u>de trouver.</u> Toutefois je ne condamne pas <u>craindre à.</u>

MALHERBE ON HIMSELF AND HIS ART

Il ne s'épargnait pas lui-même en l'art où il excellait, et disait souvent à Racan: 'Voyez-vous, monsieur, si nos vers vivent après nous, toute la gloire que nous en pouvons espérer est qu'on dira que nous avons été deux excellents arrangeurs de syllabes; que nous avons eu une grande puissance sur les paroles, pour les placer si à propos chacune en leur rang, et que nous avons tous deux été bien fous de passer la meilleure partie de notre âge en un exercice si peu utile au public et à nous-mêmes, au lieu de l'employer à nous donner du bon temps, ou à penser à l'établissement de notre fortune'. . .

Il parlait fort ingénument de toutes choses, et avait un grand mépris pour les sciences, particulièrement pour celles qui ne servent que pour le plaisir des yeux et des oreilles, comme la peinture, la musique et même la poésie, encore qu'il y fût excellent. Sur quoi Bordier se plaignant à lui qu'il n'y avait des récompenses que pour ceux qui servaient le roi dans les armées et dans les affaires d'importance, et qu'on était trop ingrat à ceux qui excellaient dans les belles-lettres, il lui répondit que c'était faire fort prudemment, et que c'était sottise de faire des vers pour en espérer autre récompense que son divertissement, et qu'un bon poète n'était pas plus utile à l'Etat qu'un bon joueur de quilles.

(Racan, *Mémoires pour la vie de M. de Malherbe*)

GUEZ DE BALZAC ON MALHERBE

(Jean-Louis Guez de Balzac, 1594-1654, essayist, critic, and major prose stylist)

Malherbe apprit à la France ce que c'était que la poésie, et parvint à contenter l'oreille, ce juge délicat et sévère. Il inventa l'art d'écrire avec pureté et bienséance, montra que l'éloquence prend sa source dans le choix des pensées et des paroles, et prouva que souvent l'heureux arrangement des choses et des mots est préférable aux choses et aux mots eux-mêmes.

Doué d'un goût pur et délicat, difficile pour lui-même, un peu trop sévère peut-être pour les autres, il réforma et dirigea l'esprit de ses contemporains avec tant de bonheur, qu'on peut le regarder comme le maître de cette foule d'auteurs distingués qui font aujourd'hui la gloire de la France.

(Balzac, *Lettres*)

THEOPHILE ON MALHERBE, AND ON HIMSELF

Or, bien que la façon de mes nouveaux écrits
Diffère du travail des plus fameux esprits,
Et qu'ils ne suivent point la trace accoutumée
Par où nos écrivains cherchent la renommée,
5   J'ose pourtant prétendre à quelque peu de bruit,
Et crois que mon espoir ne sera pas sans fruit . . .
    Imite qui voudra les merveilles d'autrui:
Malherbe a très bien fait, mais il a fait pour lui;
Mille petits voleurs l'écorchent tout en vie.
10   Quant à moi, ces larcins ne me font point d'envie.
J'approuve que chacun écrive à sa façon:
J'aime sa renommée et non pas sa leçon.
Ces esprits mendiants, d'une veine infertile
Prennent à tous propos ou sa rime ou son style,
15   Et de tant d'ornements, qu'on trouve en lui si beaux,
Joignent l'or et la soie à de vilains lambeaux,
Pour paraître aujourd'hui d'aussi mauvaise grâce
Que parut autrefois la corneille d'Horace.
Ils travaillent un mois à chercher comme à fils
20   Pourra s'apparier la rime de Memphis;
Ce Liban, ce turban et ces rivières mornes
Ont souvent de la peine à retrouver leurs bornes;
Cet effort tient leurs sens dans la confusion,
Et n'ont jamais un rais de bonne vision.
25   J'en connais qui ne font des vers qu'à la moderne,

Qui cherchent à midi Phœbus à la lanterne,
Grattent tant le français qu'ils le déchirent tout,
Blâmant tout ce qui n'est facile qu'à leur goût,
Sont un mois à connaître en tâtant la parole
30 Lorsque l'accent est rude ou que la rime est molle,
Veulent persuader que ce qu'ils font est beau,
Et que leur renommée est franche du tombeau,
Sans autre fondement sinon que tout leur âge
S'est laissé consommer en un petit ouvrage,
35 Que leurs vers dureront au monde précieux,
Pour ce qu'en les faisant ils sont devenus vieux.
De même l'araignée en filant son ordure
Use toute sa vie et ne fait rien qui dure . . .
    Je ne veux point unir le fil de mon sujet;
40 Diversement je laisse et reprends mon objet.
Mon âme, imaginant, n'a point la patience
De bien polir les vers et ranger la science.
La règle me déplaît; j'écris confusément:
Jamais un bon esprit ne fait rien qu'aisément.
45 Autrefois, quand mes vers ont animé la scène,
L'ordre où j'étais contraint m'a bien fait de la peine.
Ce travail importun m'a longtemps martyré,
Mais enfin, grâce aux Dieux, je m'en suis retiré . . .
    Je veux faire des vers qui ne soient pas contraints,
50 Promener mon esprit par des petits desseins,
Chercher des lieux secrets où rien ne me déplaise,
Méditer à loisir, rêver tout à mon aise,
Employer toute une heure à me mirer dans l'eau,
Ouïr, comme en songeant, la course d'un ruisseau,
55 Ecrire dans le bois, m'interrompre, me taire,
Composer un quatrain sans songer à le faire.
Après m'être égayé par cette douce erreur,
Je veux qu'un grand dessein réchauffe ma fureur;
Qu'une œuvre de dix ans me tienne à la contrainte
60 De quelque beau poème où vous serez dépeinte.
                    (*Elégie à une dame*, 55-60, 71-102, 115-24, 139-5〔

THEOPHILE ON STYLE

L'élégance ordinaire de nos écrivains est à plus près selon ces termes:

L'Aurore toute d'or et d'azur, brodée de perles et de rubis, paraissait aux portes de l'Orient, les étoiles éblouies d'une plus vive clarté, laissaient effacer leur blancheur, et devenaient peu à peu de la couleur du Ciel, les bêtes de la quête revenaient aux bois, et les hommes à leur travail, le silence faisait place au bruit, et les ténèbres à la lumière.

Et tout le reste que la vanité des faiseurs de livres fait éclater à la faveur de l'ignorance publique.

Il faut que le discours soit ferme, que le sens y soit naturel et facile, le langage exprès, et signifiant, les afféteries ne sont que mollesse, et qu'artifice qui ne se trouve jamais sans effort, et sans confusion. Ces larcins qu'on appelle imitation des auteurs anciens, se doivent dire des ornements qui ne sont point à notre mode. Il faut écrire à la moderne. Demosthène et Virgile n'ont point écrit en notre temps, et nous ne saurions écrire en leur siècle. Leurs livres quand ils les firent étaient nouveaux, et nous en faisons tous les jours de vieux. . . [There follow forty-seven lines of discussion of Ronsard and more recent poets] . . . Mais comme j'avais dit, il était jour. Or ces digressions me plaisent, je me laisse aller à ma fantaisie, et quelque pensée qui se présente, je n'en détourne point la plume. . .

> (From *Première Journée* (*Fragments d'une histoire comique*),
> Chapter 1 – the opening lines of the work)

THEOPHILE ON HIMSELF

Il faut avoir de la passion non seulement pour les hommes de vertu, pour les belles femmes, mais aussi pour toute sorte de belles choses. J'aime un beau jour, des fontaines claires, l'aspect des montagnes, l'étendue d'une grande plaine, de belles forêts; l'océan, ses vagues, son calme, ses rivages; j'aime encore tout ce qui touche plus particulièrement les sens: la musique, les fleurs, les beaux habits, la chasse, les beaux chevaux, les bonnes odeurs, la bonne chère: mais à tout cela, mon désir ne s'attache que pour se plaire, et non point pour se travailler; lorsque l'un ou l'autre de ces divertissements occupent entièrement mon âme, cela passe d'affection en fureur et brutalité; la passion la plus forte que je puisse avoir ne m'engage jamais au point de ne la pouvoir quitter dans un jour. Si j'aime, c'est autant que je suis aimé, et comme la Nature ni la Fortune ne m'ont pas donné beaucoup de parties à plaire, cette passion ne m'a jamais guère continué ni son plaisir ni sa peine. Je me tiens plus âprement à l'étude et à la bonne chère qu'à tout le reste. Les livres m'ont lassé quelquefois, mais ils ne m'ont jamais étourdi; et le vin m'a souvent réjoui, mais jamais enivré.

> (From *Première Journée* (*Fragments d'une histoire comique*), Chapter 2)

SAINT-AMANT ON HIS ART

Puisque, selon l'opinion du plus grand et du plus judicieux de tous les philosophes, le principal but de la poésie doit être de plaire, et que la joie est ce qui contribue le plus à l'entretien de la santé, laquelle est une chose si précieuse en cette vie, qu'elle a été préférée par les plus sages à la sagesse même, je tiens pour maxime indubitable que les plus gaies productions de ce bel art, qui, laissant les épines aux sciences, ne se compose que de fleurs, doivent être les plus recherchées et les plus chéries de tout le monde. Ce n'est pas que je veuille mettre en ce rang les bouffonneries plates et ridicules qui ne sont assaisonnées d'aucune gentillesse ni d'aucune pointe d'esprit, et que je sois de l'avis de ceux qui croient, comme les Italiens ont fait autrefois à cause de leur Bernia, dont ils adoraient les élégantes fadaises, que la simple naïveté soit le seul partage des pièces comiques. Je veux bien qu'elle y soit, mais il faut qu'elle soit entremêlée de quelque chose de vif, de noble et de fort qui la relève. Il faut savoir mettre le sel, le poivre et l'ail à propos en cette sauce; autrement, au lieu de chatouiller le goût et de faire épanouir la rate de bonne grâce aux honnêtes gens, on ne touchera ni on ne fera rire que les crocheteurs. Aussi les plus habiles de cette nation ont bien changé de sentiment depuis qu'ils ont vu *la Secchia rapita* du Tassone, où l'héroïque brille de telle sorte, et est si admirablement confondu avec le burlesque, qu'il y en a quelques uns qui, par un excès de louange, osent bien la comparer à *la Divine Jérusalem* du Tasse. Il est vrai que ce genre d'écrire, composé de deux génies si différents, fait un effet merveilleux; mais il n'appartient pas à toutes sortes de plumes de s'en mêler, et, si l'on n'est maître absolu de la langue, si l'on n'en sait toutes les galanteries, toutes les propriétés, toutes les finesses, voire même jusques aux moindres vétilles, je ne conseillerai jamais à personne de l'entreprendre. Je m'y suis plu de tout temps, parce qu'aimant la liberté comme je fais, je veux même avoir mes coudées franches dans le langage. Or, comme celui-là embrasse, sans contredit, beaucoup plus de termes, de façons de parler et de mots que l'héroïque tout seul, j'ai bien voulu en prendre la place le premier, afin que, si quelqu'un y réussit mieux après moi, j'aie à tout le moins la gloire d'avoir commencé. On peut dire qu'il est de ces pièces comme de ces balets grotesques qui, étant dancés d'ordinaire par les plus excellents baladins sur les airs du mouvement le plus admirable, plaisent plus aux spectateurs, avec leurs habits étranges, leurs masques bizarres et leurs postures merveilleuses, que ne font ces balets sérieux, ces moralités muettes, dont les démarches sont trop ajustées, et où le plus souvent il ne se voit rien de beau que l'éclat et la magnificence. . .

(From *Préface* to *Le Passage de Gibraltar. Caprice héroïcomique,* 1640)

BOILEAU ON MALHERBE
AND HIS PREDECESSORS

Durant les premiers ans du Parnasse françois,
Le caprice tout seul faisait toutes les lois.
La rime, au bout des mots assemblés sans mesure,
Tenait lieu d'ornement, de nombre et de césure.
5 Villon sut le premier, dans ces siècles grossiers,
Débrouiller l'art confus de nos vieux romanciers.
Marot bientôt après fit fleurir les ballades,
Tourna des triolets, rima des mascarades,
A des refrains réglés asservit les rondeaux,
10 Et montra pour rimer des chemins tout nouveaux.
Ronsard, qui le suivit, par une autre méthode,
Réglant tout, brouilla tout, fit un art à sa mode,
Et toutefois longtemps eut un heureux destin.
Mais sa muse, en français parlant grec et latin,
15 Vit dans l'âge suivant, par un retour grotesque,
Tomber de ses grands mots le faste pédantesque.
Ce poète orgueilleux, trébuché de si haut,
Rendit plus retenus Desportes et Bertaut.
   Enfin Malherbe vint, et, le premier en France,
20 Fit sentir dans les vers une juste cadence,
D'un mot mis en sa place enseigna le pouvoir,
Et réduisit la muse aux règles du devoir.
Par ce sage écrivain la langue réparée
N'offrit plus rien de rude à l'oreille épurée.
25 Les stances avec grâce apprirent à tomber,
Et le vers sur le vers n'osa plus enjamber.
Tout reconnut ses lois; et ce guide fidèle
Aux auteurs de ce temps sert encor de modèle.
   Marchez donc sur ses pas; aimez sa pureté,
30 Et de son tour heureux imitez la clarté.

(Art poétique, I, 113-42)

BOILEAU ON THEOPHILE

Tous les jours à la cour un sot de qualité
Peut juger de travers avec impunité;
A Malherbe, à Racan, préférer Théophile,
Et le clinquant du Tasse à tout l'or de Virgile.

(Satire IX, A son esprit, 173-76)

BOILEAU ON MALHERBE, RACAN AND SAINT-AMANT

La nature, fertile en esprits excellents,
Sait entre les auteurs partager les talents:
L'un peut tracer en vers une amoureuse flamme;
L'autre d'un trait plaisant aiguiser l'épigramme;
Malherbe d'un héros peut vanter les exploits;
Racan, chanter Philis, les bergers et les bois;
Mais souvent un esprit qui se flatte et qui s'aime
Méconnaît son génie et s'ignore soi-même:
Ainsi tel autrefois qu'on vit avec Faret
Charbonner de ses vers les murs d'un cabaret
S'en va, mal à propos, d'une voix insolente,
Chanter du peuple hébreu la fuite triomphante,
Et, poursuivant Moïse au travers des déserts,
Court avec Pharaon se noyer dans les mers.

(Art poétique, I, 13-26)

BOILEAU ON SAINT-AMANT

Soyez vif et pressé dans vos narrations;
Soyez riche et pompeux dans vos descriptions.
C'est là qu'il faut des vers étaler l'élégance;
N'y présentez jamais de basse circonstance.
N'imitez pas ce fou qui, décrivant les mers,
Et peignant, au milieu de leurs flots entr'ouverts,
L'Hébreu sauvé du joug de ses injustes maîtres,
Met, pour le voir passer, les poissons aux fenêtres;
Peint le petit enfant qui va, saute, revient,
'Et joyeux à sa mère offre un caillou qu'il tient'.
Sur de trop vains objets c'est arrêter la vue.
Donnez à votre ouvrage une juste étendue.

(Art poétique, III, 257-68)

NOTES

MALHERBE

CONSOLATION A DU PERIER, pp. 3-5

Written in 1598; a reworking of a poem written some years earlier for a different father and daughter. See Introduction, pp. xiii-xiv, xv. The poem consists of 21 quatrains of *rimes croisées*, the lines alternating between alexandrines and hexasyllables. If one detaches the general conclusion in the final three stanzas, the rest of the work falls into two exactly equal parts, lines 1-36 dealing with the precise circumstances of the girl's death, offering consolation specifically with regard to her youth, and with a first summing-up in lines 33-36; and lines 37-72 are concerned with the question of bereavement and grief in more general terms. In each case, the point is stated, then ennobled by references to classical mythology or history, while leading inexorably to the conclusion.

    25-28   The three Parcae, or Fates, span a spindleful of thread for the life of every man. When his thread came to an end, so did his life. 'La barque' is the ferry-boat of Charon, taking souls to Hades.

    29-32   Tithonus, brother of Priam of Troy, was loved by Aurora. Jupiter granted him immortality but not eternal youth; the gods finally took pity on his extreme decrepitude, and changed him into a cicada. Archemorus, son of Lycurgus, king of Thrace, died while still a small child, bitten by a snake.

    53-64   These three stanzas refer to the dramatic events of 1536, which were still just within living memory. François I's eldest son died suddenly, and it was suspected (probably wrongly) that the Emperor Charles V had had him poisoned; the Spanish army then invaded France from Italy, down the valley of the Durance, but was forced back in disarray.

    57   Alcides: i.e. Hercules.

    65-66   Malherbe had himself lost two children in infancy, Henri in 1587 and François in 1589.

DESSEIN DE QUITTER UNE DAME, p. 5

First published in 1600, but written considerably earlier, possibly in the early 1580s. Malherbe never authorized its reprinting after 1607, probably because of his dissatisfaction with certain irreducible self-imposed technical problems. See Introduction, p. xiv.

    11-12   The metaphor of Penelope's tapestry is a good example of the sort of imagery that Malherbe advocated. It dignifies the subject, yet is not too abstruse (indeed, in this case proverbial), and is appropriate on every level. The tapestry is an evocative metaphor for the poet's courtship as a laborious undertaking that constantly needs to be renewed and gets nowhere; and in addition, Penelope's motive for her subterfuge was precisely that imputed by the poet to his mistress – to put off her too ardent suitors, and delay the moment when she would have to reward their passion.

PRIERE POUR LE ROI, pp. 6-10

The king left Paris in August 1605, and ordered Malherbe to celebrate his expedition. Malherbe presented him with this poem on his return at the end of November. See Introduction, pp. xiv-xv, xvi-xvii.

    6   l'embonpoint: 'la bonne santé'.
    10   heur: 'bonne fortune'.
    22   comme: 'comment'.
    85   ennuis: 'désastres'.
    91   Henri III, last of the Valois kings, murdered in 1589.

POUR ALCANDRE, pp. 11-12

In 1609 Henri IV ('Alcandre') fell passionately in love with the young Charlotte de Montmorency. He married her to the prince de Condé, who promptly took her away from the Court, but she had to reappear for a royal wedding on 28 June; this poem celebrates her return. See Introduction, p. xiii.

    13   erreur: here means 'wandering'.

IL PLAINT LA CAPTIVITE DE SA MAITRESSE, pp. 12-14

Written at the end of 1609, when Charlotte's husband had taken her away from Court again to the Low Countries. See Introduction, p. xvii.

    14   oiseaux de Phinée: the Harpies (the Gods set them on Phineas, King of Thrace, as a punishment for his cruelty).

CHANSON (SONNET), pp. 14-15

Written on 3 June 1607 for Malherbe's mistress, the vicomtesse d'Auchy ('Caliste'). Malherbe was with the Court at Fontainebleau, Henri IV's favourite residence, which the king had greatly improved and embellished. See Introduction, p. xviii.

CHANSON, pp. 15-16

First published in 1627; probably written before 1610. The quatrains of *rimes suivies* have a most unusual metrical form, the first couplet of each stanza having nine syllables and the second couplet ten syllables. This gives a light and musical rhythm to the opening of the stanza appropriate to the cheerful amorality of the piece, and which can be the vehicle for a most effective contrast between the two halves of the stanza, as in lines 29-32, where the dancing rhythms of lines 29-30 are followed by the more ponderous regularity of the following couplet. Even in a poem such as this, Malherbe exploits his favourite technique of antithesis. One should note also, as in this stanza, the use made of the theme of nature, and the contrast between 'natural' enjoyment of sensual pleasure (in the country) and the artificial restraints of an unnatural honour (in the town).

 9-10 The sun has got his hat on. . . ! Malherbe's attempts to find a light and whimsical touch often produce rather odd results.

 12 Daphne, daughter of the river-god Peneus, who was loved by the sun-god, Apollo.

EPIGRAMMES, pp. 16-17

Two typical examples of Malherbe's barbed epigrams. The first was written after the death of the king's unpopular favourite, the Duc de Luynes, in December 1621. In the first line Malherbe is playing on the name Luynes, since 'aluine' is an old word for absinthe. The *Dictionnaire de l'Académie Française* defined it thus: 'Aluine — Herbe fort amère, qu'on nomme autrement Absynthe'. The second epigram is aimed at an unnamed lady of the Court.

PROPHETIE DU DIEU DE SEINE, p. 17

This vigorous piece of invective, written to be declaimed or sung during a *ballet de cour*, is aimed at the odious court favourite Concini, who had been killed on the king's orders on April 24, 1617.

 8 A reference to the Icarus legend.

AU ROI, pp. 17-18

Written in 1624.

5 The Hydra was a many-headed monster which grew new heads as the old ones were cut off; here, as very often, a symbol of the various outbreaks of Huguenot revolt (cf. p. 8, line 34).

POUR LE ROI, pp. 18-23

Completed in early 1628. The opening is outstandingly effective, full of urgency, movement, and strength (there are two imperative verbs in each of the first three stanzas). Implicit throughout is a double symbolic association: firstly, of Louis with Hercules (with his 'nouveau labeur') and the rebels with the Hydra whom Hercules slew in the legend, and secondly, of Louis with Jupiter (with his 'foudre') and the rebels with the Giants who revolted against him (see lines 73-92). Thereafter Malherbe skilfully varies the impact of the successive stanzas through patterns of hyperbolic statement, rhetorical questions, and accumulated imperatives (three in line 29 alone). The central theme of the power of the king is expanded through digressions on the virtue of his great agents: Richelieu (lines 37-60), the personified abstraction of Victory (lines 61 ff.), and the poet himself (lines 117-160).

5 démon: here means 'guiding spirit'.

26 A striking poetic licence, permissible at the time, but unusual in Malherbe (cf. Théophile, *Elégie*, p. 43, line 29).

35 paroître: 'paraître' in modern spelling (cf. 'françois', line 114, etc.).

47 Lynceus, one of the Argonauts, whose particular attribute was his extraordinarily sharp sight ('lynx-eyed').

59 Tiphys: pilot of the *Argo*. Syrtis and Cyaneae: legendary navigational hazards, respectively shifting sandbanks (off North Africa) and moving rocky islands (in the Black Sea).

63 Charente: the river which enters the sea not far from La Rochelle.

76-80 Briareus, Mimas, Typhon, Eurytus, Enceladus: the giants who revolted against Jupiter.

81 cette Vierge: i.e. la Victoire.

87 Phlegra: the country where the giants were destroyed by Jupiter's thunderbolts.

87 pût: present indicative of the verb *puir*, archaic for *puer* (here used to avoid the hiatus).

94 ce lâche voisin: the English, who intervened unsuccessfully on the Huguenot side at La Rochelle.

97 Megaera: one of the three Furies.

118   Aeson: father of Jason; in old age he was transformed into a youth by the magic arts of Medea.

127   i.e. from Hades (the ferry-boat of Charon) to Olympus.

153   Amphion: King of Thebes, son of Jupiter and Antiope, and one of the legendary musicians of antiquity. The magical sound of his lyre caused the stones to come together by themselves to build the walls of Thebes.

SUR LA MORT DE SON FILS, p. 24

Marc-Antoine de Malherbe was killed on 13 July 1627 in a duel with Gaspard Cauvet, baron de Bormes, and Paul de Fortia, baron de Piles. The de Fortia family had Jewish origins, hence the allusion in the last line. This poem, Malherbe's last completed work, was published in 1628. See Introduction, p. xviii.

PARAPHRASE DU PSAUME CXLV, pp. 24-25

Published in 1627. Psalm 145 in the Vulgate is numbered as Psalm 146 in Protestant versions of the psalter. See Introduction, p. xv.

THEOPHILE

LE MATIN, pp. 27-28

One of Théophile's earliest successes, rewritten several times, and also the subject of several contemporary parodies. The time-scheme is, at first sight, fairly incoherent, but most of the stanzas offer evocative, self-contained little tableaux around the general linking theme of the dawn, and there is a broad movement from cosmic and mythological fantasy to pastoral and domestic realism. The work is a tour de force of imaginative versatility, although the opening at least was later to be parodied by Théophile himself at the beginning of his *Première Journée* as an example of clichéed artificiality to be avoided by the modern school of writers (see Appendix, p. 75). However, in the poem the description is raised above the commonplace by a touch such as the dynamic and quite unexpected transitive use of the verb as the horses of the sun 'Ronflent la lumière du monde'.

13   avette: 'abeille'.

16   Mount Hymettus, near Athens, was famous for the quality and abundance of its honey.

20   Endymion: a shepherd whom the goddess Diana loved; he was eventually given immortality, but in a state of eternal sleep, and she used to visit him at night and embrace him while he slept.

21   Diana, goddess of the moon and of hunting; also given the name Hecate, and regarded (as here) as a goddess of the Underworld.

54   Ois: 'entends'.

LA SOLITUDE, pp. 28-34

Another poem that was much revised and rewritten, possibly combining three *odelettes* (lines 1-60, 61-128, 129-52). This is certainly possible, but the poem as it stands still has considerable thematic unity. Already in the first few stanzas, for example, the natural world and the mythological fantasies it stimulates are interfused with the emotions of love, and the mood of the poem is set long before the first appearance of Corine herself and its development into a more explicit love-poem.

16　Silenus: the guardian of Bacchus. Although he had the gift of prophecy, he could only exercise it when drunk, and he figures in much buffoonery on Olympus.

21　plus retenu: 'le plus retenu'.

23　There are frequent references in seventeenth century poetry to the rather gruesome story of Philomela (see Ovid, *Metamorphoses*, vi, 438-674). Philomela, daughter of Pandion, King of Athens, was raped by her brother-in-law Tereus, the brutal King of Thrace, who then cut out her tongue. In revenge, she and her sister Procne deceived him into eating his own son Ithys for dinner. When he pursued them with an axe, Tereus was changed into a hoopoe, Procne into a swallow, and Philomela into a nightingale, to lament her sorrows in the darkened woods.

36　Endymion.

44-52　The beautiful youth Hyacinthus was loved by both Apollo, the sun-god, and Boreas, god of the north wind. As Apollo and he threw the discus, the jealous Boreas blew it off course and it killed him. From his blood sprang the hyacinth flower.

144　lacs: 'liens'.

155-56　In Tasso's *Jerusalem Delivered* the hero Rinaldo is seduced into abandoning the Crusaders' army by the beautiful sorceress Armida, who keeps him in a dream-world of love.

SONNET, 'Chère Isis, tes beautés' . . ., p. 34

See Introduction, p. xxii.

SONNET, 'Vous me pressez à tort', . . ., pp. 34-35

Published in *Le Nouveau Cabinet des Muses gaillardes*, 1665; a slightly different version had appeared in *Poésies choisies de Messieurs Corneille, Boisrobert, . . ., Cinquième partie*, 1660. The delay in publication is not surprising considering the subject-matter; the poem had circulated in manuscript copies, and one ms. (of the version given here) confirms the attribution to Théophile.

EPIGRAMME, p. 35

Written before 1622, published in a *Recueil*, and, like many of Théophile's drinking songs and more ribald epigrams, not collected by the poet into editions of his works.

11   d'autant: 'abondamment'.

SATIRE PREMIERE, pp. 35-38

The beginning and end of this long and important satire are given here, but 78 rather less interesting lines have been omitted from the middle. See Introduction, pp. xxii–xxiii.

4   te point: 'te pique'.
16   un sens brutal: 'l'intelligence d'une bête'.
20   comme: 'parce qu'ils sont'.
31   pour en avoir la peur: 'de sorte qu'elle n'en a pas peur'.
32   The fable of Acheron, one of the rivers of Hades; here simply represents death.
55   Saturn is here referred to as the god of Time.
62   nous faisant du bruit: 'nous donnant du renom'.
63   plus contents: 'les plus contents'.

STANCES, pp. 38-39

The poems for Cloris were probably written from early 1620 onwards.

ELEGIE, pp. 39-41

29   'C'est une folie de chercher ailleurs qu'en nous-mêmes'.
50   'Les traits du visage ne sont même plus visibles' (Streicher).

ODE, pp. 41-44

9   délicatesses: here means that she is difficult to please, 'susceptibilités'.
46   de ta mémoire: 'du souvenir qu'on gardera de toi'.
52   gênes: 'tortures'.
58   travailles: 'fasses'.

From ELEGIE ('Souverain qui régis . . .'), pp. 44-47

This long and rather disjointed elegy contains 296 lines in all, and it has been plausibly suggested that it might be made up of a number of separate pieces (at least three) written at different dates between 1620 and 1622. This extract comprises lines 120-240 of the original. See the Introduction, p. xxi, for a comment on a couplet from the opening of the poem.

18   'qui persévérez malgré la résistance de celle que vous aimez'.

44   Si je vais: 'Si mon image se reflète'.

49   Et si: 'Et pourtant'.

59   le Démon: 'l'inspiration'. In seventeenth century poetry the word often has the sense of the Greek *daemon*, or inspiring spirit.

61   'Sans aucun effort pour forcer mon inspiration'.

65   ma frénésie: 'ma fureur poétique'.

69   The Pactolus was the legendary golden river of Lydia, which gave Croesus his vast wealth.

94   consommer: 'consumer'.

108   Streicher proposes emending 'est' to 'ist', from the archaic verb *issir*, 'to come out', 'éclore'.

ODE, p. 47

This curious piece appeared in Théophile's *Œuvres* of 1621, and accumulates signs of ill omen with an almost surrealist effect. It has been suggested that it might be a fragment of an incomplete poem on the *terreurs nocturnes* theme, of which there are other contemporary examples (most notably by Tristan l'Hermite); however, there is no evidence for this, and it stands perfectly well by itself. Several of these portents also appear in Théophile's *Pyrame et Thisbé*, IV, 2, lines 840-60 (the dream of Thisbé's mother).

6   le haut mal: epilepsy.

A MONSIEUR DE L., SUR LA MORT DE SON PERE, pp. 48-50

Found among Théophile's papers after his death, and published by Scudéry in his edition of 1632. Monsieur de L. is almost certainly Roger du Plessis, marquis de Liancourt, Théophile's friend and protector, whose father died in October 1620. See Introduction, p. xxiv.

12   Iris: i.e. the rainbow.

39   Cocytus: one of the four rivers of the underworld, which encircled Tartarus (Hades). The 'noirs flots de l'oubli' (line 50) are the waters of Lethe, where the dead drank to forget their life on earth.

REQUETE DE THEOPHILE AU ROI, pp. 51-53

Written after Théophile's arrest and imprisonment, late 1623 - early 1624. The poem contains 330 lines in all; this extract consists of lines 1-10 and 91-170.

6   mutiné: hostile.

11   cordon: the ornament worn on a hat.

31 ff.   The Jesuit Père Garasse; the next three stanzas attack the Jesuits, referring to their implication in the English Gunpowder Plot of 1605.

50   Vuital: i.e. Whitehall.

51   Père Guerin: a Minim Friar who had preached a sermon violently hostile to Théophile.

53   Tabarin: a famous farce actor (c. 1584-1633).

60   Loyola: St Ignatius Loyola, the founder of the Jesuits (as in line 32).

80   La Grève: the place in Paris where executions took place.

LA MAISON DE SILVIE, ODE III, pp. 53-56

Théophile began this series of ten odes just before his arrest, and completed it in prison. These poems, among the finest of all his work, celebrate the young Marie-Félice des Ursins, duchesse de Montmorency, and the beauties of her gardens at Chantilly (the 'Maison de Silvie' was an ornamental lodge in the park). The starting-point for this third ode is the description of the lake, 'l'étang de Silvie', watered by two streams whose dry beds can still be seen. An island in the lake contained a statue of Melicertes (or Palaemon), and a circular shelter for the swans (the 'couronne' in stanza 3). The mythological associations of the statue and the swans set the course of the poem, which becomes a subtle and evocative elaboration of the theme of metamorphosis and the poetry of moving water.

21   Melicertes was transformed by Neptune into a sea god, Palaemon.

35-40   Scylla, the sea-monster who lured mariners to their death.

57   The Nereids were sea-nymphs associated with calm water, while the Naiads were the nymphs of springs and streams.

68   Son berger: Endymion.

81   Cycnus was so upset by the death of his relative Phaeton that he metamorphosed into a swan.

93   Alan Boase has plausibly suggested that 'chacun Dieu' should be corrected to 'chacun d'eux', i.e. each of the Amours.

SAINT-AMANT

LA SOLITUDE, pp. 57-60

One of Saint-Amant's earliest poems, written before he came to Paris in 1619 or 1620. See Introduction, p. xxx. The question of priority between this poem and Théophile's is impossible to determine conclusively; much of the latter was undoubtedly written first (as early as 1612), yet in some details (such as the macabre elements of his lines 25-28) Théophile seems to be following Saint-Amant rather than *vice versa*. 'Alcidon' designates Saint-Amant's friend Charles Maignard de Bernières (named in line 71).

23-24   cf. Théophile's *Solitude*, lines 23-24.
47   glais: 'glaïeuls'.
57   alentit: 'calme', 'ralentit'.
119   lâchement: 'nonchalamment'.
123-24   The nymph Echo, rejected by Narcissus who loved only his own image, concealed herself in wild and lonely places, until at last only her voice remained.
139   Palaemon: a sea-god.

LE PASSAGE DE LA MER ROUGE, pp. 62-63

This famous description of the Israelites crossing the Red Sea, expanded from Exodus xiv, 21-22, is taken from the fifth book of Saint-Amant's epic *Moïse sauvé*, published in 1653. See Introduction, p. xxxi. Boileau's verdict on it is given in the Appendix.

3   germain: first cousin (Aaron).
16   heur: 'bonheur', happy state, as often in poetry of the period (cf. the last line of *La Solitude* above); the line evokes the Garden of Eden, here assimilated to the classical Golden Age.
30   fait la précieuse montre: 'montre comme un trésor précieux' (a bold construction).
34   exercite: 'armée' (rare).

LA PIPE, pp. 63-64

According to a (doubtful) tradition, written in a *cabaret* on Belle-Ile around 1625.

LE PARESSEUX, p. 64

Written in July-August 1630.
1   mélancolie: here in the sense defined in Furetière's *Dictionnaire*

universel (1690) as 'rêverie agréable, un plaisir qu'on trouve dans la solitude pour méditer'.
6   Frederick, Elector Palatine, irregularly elected to the throne of Bohemia, was being attacked by the Emperor Ferdinand II.
13   Jean Baudouin, prolific poet and translator, was like Saint-Amant one of the founder-members of the Académie Française.

LES GOINFRES, pp. 64-65

Probably written on Belle-Ile in 1628, once again by tradition in a *cabaret*. 'Goinfre' usually means a greedy guzzler, here extended to include all types of dissolute loose-living.

10   frise: thick woollen coat-lining. The next line means that they have sold the coat itself to buy food.

L'ENAMOURE, pp. 65-66

Written before 1629. This poem is an enjoyable burlesque of the traditional themes of the love-sick, languishing poet, exploiting techniques such as comically inappropriate juxtapositions of style and subject-matter, and drawing for much of its effect on the poet's own self-caricature.

1   j'en tiens: a slang phrase for being in love.
6   i.e. Eros the little archer, son of Venus (Virgil calls Venus *Idalia*, from Idalium on Cyprus, her birthplace).
7   Cyprine: Venus (see previous note).
10   venir à jubé: 'Obéir', 'me soumettre'.
12   revêche: coarse woollen material.
14   chevêche: 'petite chouette'.
25   petun: 'tabac' (archaic).
27   The Paris *pinte* contained almost a litre!
28   falote: 'plaisante', 'cocasse'.

L'HIVER DES ALPES, p. 66

This is the last in a series of four sonnets on the four seasons, the others being *Le Printemps des environs de Paris, L'Eté de Rome*, and *L'Automne des Canaries*. The last tercet is here given in its final version (of 1649). The first time the poem appeared, in 1631, it ended with a quite different *pointe*:

Au prix du dernier chaud ce temps m'est gracieux;
Et si la Mort m'attrape en ce chemin de verre,
Je ne saurais avoir qu'un tombeau précieux.

6   le second métal: silver.
12   l'Olympien: Jupiter (the point of the last line being that thunder-
storms are extremely rare in winter).

LE MELON, pp. 67-69

This delightful poem is too long to include in its entirety (332 lines in all,
with four more added later). These are the opening 88 lines and the final
24 lines; the central portion includes a burlesque feast of the Gods on
Olympus. Its date is uncertain, but before 1628 (death of Maillet, men-
tioned in line 105). The first part of the work is written in octosyllabic
couplets, a form which came to be particularly associated with the bur-
lesque. Both here and at the end, Saint-Amant employs with great success
a favourite technique of accumulation for comic effect.

40   Pomona, goddess of fruits and gardens.
75-76   Sugar from the Cretan sugar-canes (or possibly music from
reed-pipes).
96   petun: 'tabac'.
98   cliquettes: lepers' rattles.
103   Quinze-Vingts: an institution for the blind in Paris. Argus was
a mythological character who had a hundred eyes, of which fifty were
always open.
105   Marc de Maillet (1568-1628), a very minor poet.
106   Nicolas Faret (1596?-1646), man of letters, founder-member
of the Académie, *honnête homme*, and close friend of Saint-Amant.

SELECT BIBLIOGRAPHY

The critical studies listed below are extremely selective. Much valuable work has been produced on all three poets in recent years, both in Europe and in the United States, but the studies mentioned have been confined to a very small number for each author, and such as might be most helpful for the reader new to the field. The more general anthologies of seventeenth-century poetry are to be regarded as complements to the present edition, and many of them contain excellent introductory essays which consider the poetry of the period in a broader perspective than is possible here. The place of publication is Paris, unless otherwise stated.

A: INDIVIDUAL POETS

MALHERBE

His poems were published singly or in *Recueils collectifs* from 1587 onwards. Most important is the *Recueil des plus beaux vers* of 1627, entirely devoted to work by Malherbe and his followers, which contains 62 of his poems. First collected edition (posthumous): *Œuvres*, 1630. There were many later seventeenth-century editions, notably the critical edition by Ménage (1666).

Modern editions:
>*Œuvres de Malherbe*, ed. L. Lalanne, 5 vols, 1862-69
>*Les Poésies de Malherbe*, ed. J. Lavaud, 2 vols, 1936-37
>*Œuvres*, ed, R. Fromilhague and R. Lebègue, 2 vols, 1968
>*Œuvres*, ed. A. Adam, 1971

See:
>F. Brunot, *La Doctrine de Malherbe*, 1891
>R. Fromilhague, *Malherbe, technique et création poétique*, 1954
>R. Fromilhague, *La Vie de Malherbe: apprentissages et luttes*, 1954
>F. Ponge, *Pour un Malherbe*, 1965

THEOPHILE DE VIAU

Poems in *Recueils collectifs*, 1619-22. *Œuvres*, 1621, 1622, 1623, 1625, 1626, and many later seventeenth-century editions.

Modern editions:
    Œuvres poétiques, ed. J. Streicher, 2 vols, 1951-58.
    Œuvres complètes, ed. G. Saba, Rome, 4 vols, 1978-87.

See:

    A. Adam, *Théophile de Viau et la libre-pensée française en 1620*, 1935
    C. L. Gaudiani, *The Cabaret Poetry of Théophile de Viau, Texts and Traditions*, Tübingen and Paris, 1981

SAINT-AMANT

Œuvres, 1629, *Suite des Œuvres*, 1631, *Seconde Partie des Œuvres*, 1643; many subsequent editions, and longer poems published separately. Also: *Moïse sauvé, Idylle héroïque*, 1653; *Dernier Recueil de diverses poésies*, Rouen, 1658.

Modern editions:
    Œuvres complètes, ed. C.-L. Livet, 2 vols, 1855
    Œuvres, ed. J. Lagny and J. Bailbé, 5 vols, 1967-79

See:

    F. Gourier, *Etude des œuvres poétiques de Saint-Amant*, Geneva, 1961
    J. Lagny, *Le Poète Saint-Amant*, 1964
    C. D. Rolfe, *Saint-Amant and the Theory of 'Ut pictura poesis'*, London, 1972
    A. Rathé, 'Saint-Amant, poète du "caprice" ', *XVIIe Siècle*, 118-19 (1978), pp. 229-44

B: ANTHOLOGIES

M. Allem, *Anthologie poétique française, XVIIe siècle*, new ed. (Garnier-Flammarion), 2 vols, 1965

D. Aury, *Anthologie de la poésie religieuse française*, 1945

A. Blanchard, *Trésor de la poésie baroque et précieuse (1550-1650)*, 1969.

A. M. Boase, *The Poetry of France, Volume II, 1600-1800*, London, 1973

A. Cart, *La Poésie française au XVIIe siècle, 1594-1640*, 1939

J.-P. Chauveau, *Anthologie de la poésie française du XVIIe siècle*, 1987

F. Duviard, *Anthologie des poètes français (XVIIe siècle)*, 1947

F. Fleuret and L. Perceau, *Satires françaises du XVIIe siècle*, 2 vols, 1923

T. Maulnier, *Poésie du XVIIe siècle*, 1945

T. Maulnier and D. Aury, *Poètes précieux et baroques*, Angers, 1941

O. de Mourgues, *An Anthology of French Seventeenth-Century Lyric Poetry*, Oxford, 1966

P. Olivier, *Cent Poètes précieux ou burlesques du XVIIe sièle*, 1898

R. Picard, *La Poésie française de 1640 à 1680*, 2 vols, 1964

J. Rousset, *Anthologie de la poésie baroque française*, 2 vols, 1961

D.L. Rubin, *La Poésie française du premier XVIIe siècle: textes et contextes*, Tübingen, 1986

A.-M. Schmidt, *L'Amour Noir, poèmes baroques*, Monaco, 1959

A. J. Steele, *Three Centuries of French Verse, 1511-1819*, Edinburgh, 1950

C: GENERAL CRITICISM

A. Adam, *Histoire de la littérature française du XVIIe siècle*, 5 vols, 1948-56

Y. Fukui, *Raffinement précieux dans la poésie française du XVIIe siècle*, 1964

Th. Gautier, *Les Grotesques*, 1844 (an interesting Romantic view of, among others, Théophile and Saint-Amant)

H. Lafay, *La Poésie française du premier dix-septième siècle*, 1976

O. de Mourgues, *Metaphysical, Baroque, and Précieux Poetry*, Oxford, 1953

J.-C. Payen and J.-P. Chauveau, *La Poésie des origines à 1715* (Collection 'U'), 1968

J. Rousset, *La Littérature de l'âge baroque en France*, 1953

J. Rousset, *L'Intérieur et l'extérieur*, 1968

D. L. Rubin, *The Knot of Artifice: A Poetic of the French Lyric in the Early 17th Century*, Columbus, Ohio, 1981

R. Winegarten, *French Lyrical Poetry in the Age of Malherbe*, Manchester, 1954

D: THE TECHNIQUES OF FRENCH VERSE

P. Delbouille, *La Sonorité des vers*, 1961

F. Deloffre, *Le Vers français*, 1973

Th. Elwert, *La Versification française*, 1965

P. Giraud, *La Versification*, 1970

M. Grammont, *Petit Traité de versification française* (Collection 'U'), 1965 (first published 1908)

M. Grammont, *Le Vers français, ses moyens d'expression, son harmonie*, 2nd ed., 1913

R. Lewis, *On Reading French Verse*, Oxford, 1982

C. Scott, *French Verse-Art. A Study*, Cambridge, 1980

C. Scott, *The Riches of Rhyme: Studies in French Verse*, Oxford, 1988

M. Souriau, *L'Evolution du vers français au dix-septième siècle*, 1893

INDEX OF FIRST LINES

Lightning Source UK Ltd.
Milton Keynes UK
15 May 2010

154230UK00001B/22/P